DEATH COMES HOME

DEATH
COMES HOME

by

SIMON STEPHENS

MOWBRAYS

LONDON & OXFORD

*Printed in Great Britain
at The Pitman Press*

(Paper) ISBN 0 264 64559 6
(Boards) ISBN 0 264 64604 5

First published 1972 *by A. R. Mowbray & Co Ltd
The Alden Press, Osney Mead, Oxford, OX2 0EG*

CONTENTS

	Preface	*page*	ix
	Foreword by Dr Hugh Jolly		xi
1	Into Quarantine		1
2	A Profound Silence		21
3	The Great Unmentionable		33
4	Reactions to Grief		43
5	The Bereaved and the Caring Team		54
6	A Ministry of Compassion		74
7	In Search of a Solution		87
8	The Christian Hope		94
	Anthology		101
	Bibliography		113

TO

SIMON MARK

PREFACE

THIS BOOK has been written in the hope that those who read it, whether doctor or nurse, parish priest or those involved in the sorrow of others, will be prompted to examine their own attitude to death and the quality of their own ministry to the bereaved. I hope that the true story of Margaret and Peter will prompt each one of us to face death and bereavement more realistically. In our acceptance of its inevitability, we shall discover that freedom of spirit which only comes when fear of death has been resolved.

I wish to record my sincere appreciation of the help and encouragement which I have received from the Staff and patients of the Coventry & Warwickshire Hospital, Canon William Purcell of Worcester Cathedral, the Revd Joseph Humble, my Vicar and Mrs Lillian Milligan, and my secretary—without whose help this book could not have been written.

Finally, it should be made clear that the incidents recorded in this book did not occur in the Coventry & Warwickshire Hospital nor in any of the other hospitals with which I am closely associated. Joe, Nurgant and Peter Robinson were all real life people—but their names have been changed.

Leamington Spa   Simon Stephens
Spring 1972

FOREWORD

PETER and Margaret lost their much loved son Joe. Every year, in Britain, 27,000 homes mourn the death of a child. What then happened to Peter and Margaret was the same as happens to the majority of bereaved parents; they were left alone, being put into quarantine just as if they were lepers.

Far from just not being helped by their neighbours in the friendly community where they lived, Peter and Margaret actually suffered at their hands—they were shunned. Their friends did what they could to avoid them and the seat next to Peter in the factory bus was always left empty.

What is it that produces this extraordinary reaction among friends? In days gone by, when death was more of an every day affair, it could be discussed without embarrassment; it still is in developing countries. But in Western society today, death, unlike sex, has become the taboo subject. Not only is it not talked about, but steps are taken to hide its traces. In some children's wards or classrooms, beds and desks are re-arranged to hide the absentee.

Is there anything we can do to help? Simon Stephens is a young parish priest, but with considerable experience of the problem. As a hospital chaplain he has allowed himself to become deeply involved in the problems facing bereaved parents. It is from this experience that he examines the reasons for the behaviour of neighbours and friends, and points the way to the answer.

Bereaved parents need to talk of the child they have lost, not to be surrounded by a conspiracy of silence. On the day of Joe's funeral no one mentioned his name, not even the parson. If they are to talk, they need someone to listen to them—a compassionate listener. It is this which has led the author to found the Society of the Compassionate Friends. Its members are bereaved parents, who, having worked through their own grief now feel able to help others in the same position as themselves.

This is a book for everyone, though perhaps particularly for those whose work is to care for others—doctors, nurses, clergy, social workers and many more. For too long the care of the bereaved has not entered into their training. Doctors, particularly, while being well trained to cure have been poorly trained to care. It is easier to avoid the bed of a child whom you cannot cure than to find something new to say to him or to his parents. The conspiracy of silence is likely to begin even before bereavement.

Dr Hugh Jolly,
Consultant Paediatrician, Charing Cross Hospital

INTO QUARANTINE

My brothers stand aloof from me,
and my relations take care to avoid me.
My kindred and my friends have all gone away
and the guests in my house have forgotten me.

Job 19. 13, 14 J.B.

It was Autumn. September's first golden leaves skipped along Mickleforth Terrace as if anxious to join their colleagues on a large bonfire, which the 'gang', in anticipation of a dry November night were building on a bomb-site further down the street. Windows shook, and in the distance the familiar rattle of milk bottles heralded the arrival of the roundsman's float. A leaden sky greeted those on the early morning shift and their footsteps echoed as they made their way to the factory bus. There was nothing special about Mickleforth Terrace. It's grey flag-stoned pavements provided little contrast to the blackened homes towering above them. The only relief came from an odd assortment of flower boxes, where green fingers bribed the poor earth to produce just a few blooms once a year.

It was a happy street and those who lived in these terraced houses had shared their joys and their frustrations for many a generation. On Saturday the street re-echoed to the cheers from football enthusiasts encouraging their home team to victory on the nearby ground. On Sunday nothing stirred to disturb the slumber of these families until just before noon when the inevitable football bounced into action at the far end of the street. But then the Williams had always been light sleepers. The whole street knew that!

But this morning was no ordinary Monday morning. House lights had been burning from an extraordinarily early hour and from some of those homes came the excited chatter of children as they stirred their slumbering parents into action. New, shining satchels came under the close scrutiny of their proud owners and, in one home at least, a pair of new shoes squeaked their way—ever so softly—upstairs for their debut before wide-eyed brothers and sisters. Yes, it was the beginning of the new school term. That long awaited day after the seemingly endless weeks of the summer holidays. It was an important day. It meant new classes, new friends and even new schools, and best of all the school play and Christmas. So it really was a very important Monday morning.

But never had a morning been so important to a family as it was to the Robinsons. After months, even years of hard work and self-sacrifice, the Great Day for which the whole family had waited so long had arrived. Lights at 22, Mickleforth Terrace had gone on before any others in the street and they had been quickly followed by those at No 23 who found further sleep impossible with such noisy neighbours. Today was to be their day, or more precisely, their Joe's. Joseph, or 'Joe' as he was better known to the 'gang', was just eleven years old and the eldest of the Robinsons three children. There was the baby Clare, eighteen months old and a bundle of fun who more often than not served as an alarm clock for those who lived at Nos 21 and 23. Then there was John, a nine year-old who had won the respect of the entire Mickleforth Terrace through his ownership of an autographed photograph of the League Champions. And then there was Joe, dark haired and an accomplished footballer despite his years. A boy with many friends and many ambitions. Just one boy among the many boys who played football down the street.

His parents, Margaret and Peter, had moved to the

Terrace some ten years ago, when Joe was still a babe in arms, in search of a new life when the mine in which Peter Robinson had worked since leaving school had closed. The Robinsons had moved North after generations of their family had worked in the coal fields of South Wales. It was a tremendous wrench, but the couple felt that their new life in the terrace would provide their son with the opportunities that they themselves had never been able to enjoy. Peter Robinson secretly hoped that Joe would follow him to the pit face. But after all he was still only a child and whereas Peter had had no other alternative but to go down the pit, he wanted to make quite sure that at least his boy would have a choice. So in pursuit of the privilege of choice the Robinsons had moved North, where they quickly became accepted as members of the Mickleforth 'community'.

As Joe grew up, his parents spent what time they could spare encouraging his interests. His thirst for the bloody battles of English history was wetted by the occasional expedition which he made with his father to the local museum, and not an evening passed without a tea-time discussion on the progress he was making with his school work. Reports from his form mistress Miss Rutter were encouraging: 'Joseph is a kind well mannered boy. He tries hard in all subjects, although he finds concentration for any length of period difficult.' In the light of this and his middle of the class position, his parents were well satisfied.

And then the unexpected happened. A letter arrived from the school suggesting that if his parents were agreeable, Joseph should be a candidate for a scholarship examination to St John's Boys College in the neighbouring town of Darlington. When Margaret and Peter had read the letter they found it difficult to hide their excitement. '. . . . Exam. Scholarship to St John's for their boy Joe. Was it possible?'

They discussed the letter with Joe who shared their enthusiasm. 'Why not, Mum! Richard and Andrew from my class are going in for the exam! Why shouldn't I?' That sealed the matter. Joe was to sit the examination! That winter the football remained in it's cupboard beneath the stairs as Joe, in the company of his Dad, prepared for the May examination. Every waking moment of the day was spent absorbing a long list of Joe's favourite dates. 'What happened in 1066?' Indeed, it seemed as if that day in May would never, never come. But at last the waiting was over and in the company of his two class-mates Joe sat the two and a half hour examination paper. As he recalled sometime later, 'I was not the least bit afraid.' In that time, he crammed as much information as his memory would permit into his answers and when the final bell went, he put down his much chewed pen and sat back with an air of satisfaction at a job well done. 'Well, that's that!'

The weeks following the examination were just as demanding as those which preceded it. The arrival of the morning post became the great event of the day. Every post-mark was scrutinised and the familiar broken 'T' of the school secretary's typewriter was eagerly searched for. And when it became clear that the letter was not in that post, the family would reluctantly return to work—even though waiting another twenty-four hours with so much suspense seemed almost impossible. Days passed into weeks. Would that letter ever come? Secretly in their hearts Margaret and Peter resigned themselves to a 'failure' slip. It couldn't be helped. Their boy had done his best and that's all there was to it. Despite his parents flagging enthusiasm, Joe continued to wait impatiently for the letter from the school. Hadn't Miss Rutter told him that he could do it if he really tried? And how he had tried! Night after night he had deserted the Mickleforth 'gang' and their football for the kitchen table groaning

4

under the weight of school text books. And anyway, he comforted himself, the answer he gave to the question about the historical significance of 1066 was surely worth a pass. It must be worth a pass!

But as the weeks dragged on Joe too began to fear the worst, and although he never mentioned his feeling to his parents he began to fear the arrival of the postman. What would his parents say to him, and even more important what could he say to them? The waiting seemed interminable.

And then quite suddenly, one morning, it arrived! There it was on the door mat. The broken 'T' boldly identifying it's source as the school typewriter. The Robinsons found it difficult to conceal their anxiety! What could they say to Joe if he had . . .? With the family around the kitchen table, Peter Robinson tore open the envelope. He glanced hurriedly through the letter and with expressionless face he handed it to his wife. 'Dear Mr and Mrs Robinson,' the letter read, 'You will be pleased to learn that as a result of the examination which Joseph sat last May, he has been awarded a place at St John's College. We hope that he will be very happy in his new school and. . . .' Margaret left off reading. 'You've passed!' she exclaimed,' 'You've passed the examination.' Immediately the whole house was in an uproar and their neighbours at Nos 21 and 23 guessed that the long awaited news had arrived. No breakfast was eaten that morning. Who could possibly eat a breakfast under such circumstances! Peter Robinson left the house a good ten minutes early. What news he would have to tell the lads at pit No 3. His lad Joe was to go to college. His lad! That morning the old pit bus which stopped at the end of the Terrace felt like a limousine. What a day it was going to be. Meanwhile, back at home, Joe was summoning the 'gang' to tell them his good news. 'I've passed Bobby, I've got a place at St John's.' And what would Miss Rutter say when he told her the news?

5

positively Joe glowed in anticipation of the honours which would be heaped upon him that day at school. It would certainly be mentioned in the morning Assembly and in the classroom afterwards, and, who knows, there just might be a book prize for him at the school's annual prize-giving. As for Margaret Robinson, well as soon as her household chores had been completed she was off to the phone box on the corner. It was going to be a busy morning. Her parents would just have to hear the news and then there were Joe's god-parents. And then of course there were all the other relations, they would have to hear as well!

The months that followed Joe's scholarship to St John's College saw much activity at No 22 Mickleforth Terrace. There were books to be bought, and Peter Robinson took advantage of offers of overtime to save sufficient money to buy Joe's new school uniform. There was the cap and blazer, the new grey flannels (Joe didn't care much for those) and the white shirts to go with them. Yes, the school uniform was going to be an expensive item. Not to mention the many other requirements specified on a long list which had recently arrived from the new school. Changing schools was a costly affair, but if it was for their Joe, then the personal sacrifices made were well worth it.

The summer term passed by surprisingly quickly and, as Joe had expected, a prize came his way at the end of term. What glory for him! He was sad of course, to be leaving his old school behind. He had been so happy there and Miss Rutter really had been such a good friend. But any lingering sadness or regret was quickly forgotten in his enthusiasm to join his class-mates Richard and Andrew at St John's. There was of course no summer holiday for the Robinson family that year. There were far too many other demands on their pockets. But there would always be another year and opportunities for other holidays. Meanwhile, Joe modelled his new school uniform before rows of admiring aunts and uncles. Their admiration alone was sufficient reward to Margaret and Peter for the hard work which they had put into the last few months. Not a day passed without Joe fondly handling the new leather satchel which an admiring grandfather had given him. It really was beautiful, and on the flap his initials 'JR' had been embossed in gold.

And then at long last, after months of waiting and endless preparation ('Surely, there had never been quite such a long summer holiday, thought Joe') the great day came. So on that Monday morning, as September leaves sought to banish all memories of warm summer days, the Robinson family rose especially early to ensure that Joseph got off to a good start at his new school. From early morning, Joe's new shoes had been squeaking their way around the house as he admired his new uniform in the bathroom mirror and meticulously packed his satchel. Once again his breakfast was barely touched and at 8.15 a.m. to a chorus of 'Good Luck' from the entire family, Joe left No 22 and rather self-consciously made his way down the street. How his shoes squeaked and how nervous he felt! But why was he worrying? There would be many other new boys, or 'new youths' as they were called, and on the bus he would be meeting Richard and Andrew from his old class. Surely they must be feeling just like him!

So Joe began his new life at St John's. During his first week at school the most important part of the day came when he returned home in the evening. Sitting at the kitchen table and surrounded by his family he would talk about the day's happenings and the new friends made. 'Yes,' said Joe, we've got our own swimming pool *and* four football pitches!' And how many are there in your class? Who is your form-master? How much homework will you have to bring home in the evenings? So question followed question and with boundless enthusiasm Joe described the merits of his new school. Indeed it was not long before the whole of Mickleforth Terrace knew by heart every detail of his new life at St John's. Every day he brought home new and exciting stories about what he had seen and done. How Margaret and Peter revelled in all this! This was one of the happiest periods of their lives and they both felt a tremendous sense of achievement.

And then tragedy struck! During his second week at school Joe became rather listless. He wasn't quite his normal happy self. He was paler than usual and his meals both at home and at school were left almost untouched. This change in him did not pass unnoticed by Margaret and Peter. But they attributed his loss of appetite to the difficult period of re-adjustment which many youngsters go through when they move from the familiar territory of the Junior school to the rather impersonal system of secondary education. Hadn't they themselves gone through just such an emotional upheaval many years before? They too recalled those secret fears which accompanied them during those transitory years. There lad was OK. He would soon settle down.

But this was not to be, and before the end of the week Joe complained to his parents about increasing pain in his left side. He said it made him feel sick, and he just didn't feel like eating. Indeed, he felt far from well and couldn't face school tomorrow. Margaret and Peter were not unduly anxious. 'A warm bed and a good night's sleep with the aid of a tablet would do him the world of good.' Next morning, however, Joe had not improved. His face was marked by lack of sleep and he complained that the pain in his side made him feel very sick. He was told to stay in bed and his mother, en route to the Junior school with his brother, rang the family doctor and asked him if he could come and see her son. 'It's just a precaution. To make sure that there is nothing seriously wrong', she said as she walked back home with a neighbour from the phone box on the corner.

Within two hours, the doctor who had cared for the Robinson family since their arrival at Mickleforth Terrace came to No 22. His re-assuring smile and warm words put to flight any secret anxieties which Margaret may have had. 'How's he getting on at his new school, Mrs Robinson?' he asked as she lead him up the narrow staircase to the back bedroom which Joe shares with his brother. 'He'll do well there and be a credit to the whole street'. The door was opened, revealing young Joe almost hidden beneath a mountain of blankets in a bed on the far side of the room. Joe was feeling rather sorry for himself. The gnawing pain in his side had kept him awake most of the night. Indeed, he recalled that he had been able to follow the whole of the milkman's 5 a.m. round up the Terrace. The clink of milk bottles on the well-scrubbed door steps echoing time and time again. As the doctor came across the room with his mother, Joe reflected to himself that he had never really liked doctors. Their probing fingers were always cold, as were their instruments. And as for their medicines, well that was another matter! But if this one could remove the ache in his left side, then he was very happy to see him. As the mother stood back, the doctor examined Joe. In a minute he straightened his back, his diagnosis made. 'It's appendicitis Mrs Robinson. Nothing to worry about too much, but I think we ought to get him into hospital as soon as possible. Make sure he has nothing else to eat or drink, meanwhile I'll return to the Surgery and arrange for his admission to hospital in Darlington. Please don't worry. The lad will be quite safe in our hands.' With these words the doctor disappeared down the staircase, leaving Margaret sitting in numbed silence by Joe's bedside. 'Hospital, appendicitis, a possible operation'; she was beginning to panic until she realised that Joe was searching

9

her face for some sign, some words of re-assurance and comfort. She checked herself, 'Don't worry Joe, both your father and I have had to go into hospital for appendicitis. It must be in the family! They won't keep you there long and they'll get rid of that pain.' To avoid answering questions which she felt she could not answer, Margaret hurried downstairs. She felt quite sure that next door would look after Clare and provide John with his lunch, whilst she accompanied Joe to the district hospital. Meanwhile she busied herself packing a small suitcase. 'He'll need his dressing gown, a pair of slippers, another pair of pyjamas and of course his sponge bag', she thought to herself as she gathered the items together. 'And perhaps they'll let me ring Peter from the hospital.'

The case was hardly packed, when the ambulance arrived! The arrival of an ambulance in Mickleforth Terrace was always an important event. Within minutes of it's arrival outside No 22 a little group of neighbours had gathered. 'It's Joe,' said one of their number,' he's got appendicitis, he has. Poor kid and only just begun at his new school.' Ignoring their chatter and sympathetic glances, the ambulance crew pushed passed them and entered the house. 'He's in the back bedroom,' said Margaret, 'please be careful with him. He's in so much pain.' With characteristic good humour and firm friendliness the crew lifted Joe on to the stretcher. 'Now hang on lad, as we take you downstairs. You're going to be alright. Not nervous are you?' Joe shook his head. With Margaret following behind, carrying Joe's suitcase, the little procession left the house. The group of Terrace women who had gathered, respectfully drew back. 'Don't worry Joe,' one called out,' you'll soon be back with us.' But the boy was far from worrying. He just wanted to get rid of that beastly pain in his side. Another neighbour, seeing the anxiety in his mother's face, gave her arm a re-assuring squeeze.

Margaret smiled, her confidence restored, and followed Joe into the ambulance.

Within a very few minutes the ambulance arrived at Greenhill District Hospital. Suddenly, Margaret found herself in a strange new world. A nurse met the stretcher from the ambulance. She was smiling. 'I wish I had her confidence', thought Margaret. Whilst his mother was assisting a clerk at the Reception Desk to fill an Admission Form, Joe was wheeled into a special side ward. Curtains were drawn about him and momentarily he was left quite alone. The smell of disinfectant reminded him of the laboratory in his new school and just as he was about to begin a more detailed inspection of the cubicle in which he lay, the curtains parted. 'Hello Joe,' remarked the junior houseman who came to his side carrying a sheaf of notes, 'now let's see what we can do for this pain of yours.' His fingers were not as cold as those of his own doctor back at the Terrace, thought Joe. But his diagnosis was the same. With great care the doctor explained to Joe at some length what was causing him so much discomfort. His appendix was so inflamed that it would have to be removed. It was only a small operation and he need have nothing to worry about. Joe was not quite so sure! Meanwhile, a nurse was matching his blood group and the children's ward had been asked to prepare a bed for him. Upstairs, the theatre was standing by for an emergency appendicectomy.

Within a few minutes Margaret had contacted her husband at the pit head. She was then re-united with Joe and accompanied him in the lift to his ward which was on the third floor. Here she met the Ward Sister and remained in her office whilst Joe was transferred from the trolley to his hospital bed. 'What a vast place this is,' thought Margaret, 'so impersonal. There seem to be so many people, so many different uniforms and doors and staircases everywhere.' For the first time Margaret felt alone. But the voices of other children in the ward interrupted her thoughts, as did the Ward Sister: 'We have decided to operate early this afternoon and we can foresee no complications. But I am sure you wish to stay with Joseph until he goes down to the theatre. Nurse will take you to him.' Margaret was taken to the ward's second cubicle and in the bed nearest the window she found Joe. Even though he was eleven years of age, he looked very small in that large hospital bed. Indeed, although he would never admit it, he felt rather small and insignificant. If only he had his new cap and blazer! Then at least people would know that he attended St John's College. 'And there can't be many boys which do in this hospital', he thought. He didn't even have the security of his own pyjamas—but had been dressed in a long white gown. It made him feel rather foolish, but he was thankful that neither Richard nor Andrew could see him. What would they have said! But these thoughts were abruptly interrupted, 'What's your name?' asked the boy in the bed opposite him. 'Joe Robinson,' he replied, 'What's yours?' 'Mike Henstock,' the lad answered. 'What have you come in for?' In an air of self importance, Joe replied, 'My appendix. They're taking it out sometime this afternoon.' At the mention of 'appendix' Mike promptly pulled up his pyjama jacket. 'They did mine as well,' he said. 'There'll be a scar there when they take the dressing off.' Joe didn't quite know whether he wanted a scar or not, but he liked Mike Henstock and thought he would be good fun.

Whilst the boys were talking, Margaret was looking about her. The ward was large and airy. A large tank of tropical fish stood on a table in the middle of the ward and at the far end some book shelves made up the 'Children's Library'. From where she was sitting she could see several other children and their cheerful faces re-assured her that there was nothing to worry about.

Time passed quickly, and whilst Mike and Joe were still discussing the merits of their own schools a distant rumble heralded the arrival of the theatre trolley. Strong but gentle hands transferred Joe from his bed to the trolley and with a thumbs-up sign to his newly found friend he disappeared from sight. Meanwhile, Margaret Robinson at the suggestion of a sensitive ward Sister, who knew from experience just how long two hours of surgery can seem to the patient's mother, left the hospital to do some of the family shopping in the nearby shops. There were vegetables to be bought. John required a new pair of shorts for his PE lessons and the rates had to be paid. However, her thoughts were far away from such mundane matters and within half an hour she found herself back in the ward and waiting! Mike questioned her about Joe's skill with a football. 'Was he as good as he said he was, or was he just boasting?' But Margaret scarcely heard these questions. She was thinking. Thinking of Joe and of what was happening to him at that very moment. Of course the operation would be a success! Thousands are performed daily. Why shouldn't it be a success? It's just got to be a success! But sometimes, and an icy chill spread across her back, sometimes the unexpected happens. Oh God, why is Joe so long in returning from the theatre? If anything happens to him, I'll . . . Just as she was about to be overcome by an indescribable panic her thoughts were interrupted by a familiar sound. Within a few seconds the trolley with her Joe re-appeared in the ward. 'What a fool she had been to think that. . . .' Carefully, the still semi-conscious boy was lifted from the trolley and placed back into his bed. 'He looks pale,' thought Margaret, 'but then that was to be expected. Who wouldn't?' At that moment Sister re-appeared. The operation had been a success, she assured Margaret Robinson, but it might be quite some time before Joe was fully conscious. If she wanted to, suggested Sister, she could go home now and return later this evening by which time Joe would be able to appreciate her presence. Margaret however, recalling a childhood fright when she had awoken from an anaesthetic to find herself almost alone in a strange hospital ward, decided to stay at Joe's side with the nurse until he awoke. Half an hour later, her wait was rewarded. Joe opened his eyes, smiled at his mother in recognition and then went into a natural sleep. Re-assured that her boy was on the mend, Margaret left the hospital and began the journey home. How quickly the day had passed! She still had so much to do. Household chores remained undone. Then there was Clare to be fed and John would soon be returning home for his tea. However, later that evening in the company of Peter she would return to the hospital to see how Joe was progressing.

Back in Mickleforth Terrace there was a steady stream of callers to No 22 for the remainder of that afternoon. Baskets of fruit, flowers ('funny things to give a boy' thought Margaret) and comics filled the front room. Even the 'gang' clubbed together to buy Joe a new football shirt. 'Give him our regards won't you Mrs Robinson, and tell him that we hope to see him back in the street soon.' Secretly, both Margaret and Peter were thrilled by these spontaneous acts of kindness. But they were not really surprised ... after all Joe was their extra-special boy. Later that evening, as the neighbours minded the younger children, the Robinsons returned to the hospital weighed down with presents. But Joe was still very sleepy, and Sister suggested that they return the following day when their son would be more like his old self.

Next day Margaret Robinson returned to the hospital and as she walked up the drive she congratulated herself on having such kind and understanding neighbours. Once again they were going to care for Clare and provide John with his lunch. 'It's good to know who your friends are during times of crisis such as this,' she thought as she pushed her way through the swing doors. Within minutes she found herself back again in the ward and as she made her way to the second cubicle, Sister called her back to her office. 'Mrs Robinson, may I have a word with you for a minute?' Margaret retraced her steps. 'I'm afraid Joseph is still not quite his normal self. Sometimes it takes one child longer than another to recover from the post-operative side effects. But don't worry too much. He'll be all right and doctor will see him on his rounds.'

Trying to conceal her anxiety, Margaret moved down the ward to her son's bedside. Joe was awake and in a dreamy sort of way he smiled at his mother. It was good to see her! 'Hello Joe, are you feeling better this morning?' The boy nodded. His mother emptied the contents of her shopping bag on to the locker by his bedside. 'These have come from Mrs Williams at No 32.' she said placing a roll of comics on his bed. 'And these from the Barwells . . . and just look at this, the "gang" have clubbed together to buy you this new shirt.' But as Margaret looked up she saw that 'far away' look in Joe's eyes. He hadn't heard a thing she was saying. 'He's obviously still very tired after his operation', thought Margaret as she packed the remainder of the neighbours' gifts away into his locker and prepared to spend several hours sitting quietly at his bedside. At least she would have Mike's company. So the morning passed without event. The hum of a busy ward routine filled her ears. In the next cubicle, Miss Crawford, head teacher of the hospital school, was coaching a young girl in mathematics for her eleven plus. At the far end of the ward, Sister was giving her student nurses a lecture on the post-operative care of patients.

At 2 p.m. the doctor made his ward round in the company of Sister and several junior housemen. 'Do you mind standing outside just a minute whilst the doctor examines

Joe?' asked a nurse. Margaret Robinson was pleased to have the opportunity to stretch her legs. She was surprised just how tiring hospital visiting could be and she took advantage of the doctor's round to slip downstairs for a quick cup of tea at the WVS canteen. Meanwhile, with the curtains pulled around Joe's bed, a hurried conference took place in hushed tones. Downstairs Margaret pondered over a cup of tea. Within minutes she had returned to the ward. The curtains around her son's bed parted and with a smile in her direction, but without stopping, the party moved on to the next bed. Not a word was said! The day passed uneventfully. Joe occasionally stirred, but for the most part he lay as if in a daze. Saying very little and eating nothing. Margaret was worried and she thought Joe's nurse was worried too. Why else did she prevent her from asking those questions she really wanted to ask? And whenever she got around to mentioning Joe, nurse was suddenly called away to another bed. But hadn't Sister told her not to worry and surely if there had been anything amiss the doctor would have spoken to her on his rounds. Dismissing these secret anxieties from her mind Margaret Robinson returned to Mickleforth Terrace where two hungry children and a husband demanded her love and attention for the remainder of the evening. But she was still worried and when she went up to bed later that night she shared these fears with Peter. But he was no alarmist, he never had been. 'If there was anything wrong with our Joe, anything seriously wrong,' he assured Margaret, 'they would tell us. You worry far too much!' In Peter's company the size of those secret fears of hers diminished and within a short time they were both asleep.

Next day, Joe's condition remained unchanged. Mike thought his newly found friend poor company, but then he didn't really mind as he would soon be going home. Sister, however was rather more concerned, indeed if her nurses but knew it she was really quite worried about the Robinson boy in the second cubicle. She would ask the doctor on his rounds that morning to have a special look at Joe. But as yet she was unable to identify any specific symptoms which could give cause for anxiety. Later that morning, doctor on his rounds made another careful examination of Joe. He obtained a second opinion and then went to confer with Sister in her office. 'Joe Robinson's condition does give me some cause for worry Sister. But I agree with you, I can identify no specific symptoms which at the moment would make some form of diagnosis possible. Please see that he is carefully observed during the next twenty-four hours and ensure that all nursing care is given.' That afternoon Margaret and Peter visited the hospital together. Joe was pale and drowsy and he didn't seem to recognise them. Although he never mentioned it to his wife, Peter Robinson found it difficult to recognise the pale and very small boy who lay in the bed before him, as his son Joe. Somehow, in some indefinable way, he had changed. Something was wrong and they knew it. After much hesitation, because they knew what a busy person she was, the Robinsons approached Sister's office. She had been expecting them, but what could she say? She was just as worried as they were about Joe. But it would not do for them to know that. And besides, she was short-staffed this afternoon and she was expecting several admissions. This was no time for a lengthy conversation! 'We're sorry to disturb you Sister, but we're worried about Joe. He's not his normal self. Far from it in fact', said Peter Robinson. 'Now don't worry', Sister said to the worried parents, 'he's going to be alright. I am sure that he could be more like his old self if he wanted to.' And in a desperate effort to bring the conversation to a speedy conclusion, she remarked 'He's really behaving rather like a spoiled child! Now please excuse me!' Almost immediately she regretted the words which had slipped out, but it was too late and there was no turning back. She smiled weakly and said, 'If you have any other worries, please come and see me again.' Something seemed to explode inside Margaret. 'Joe spoilt. Never! But perhaps he was playing-up just a little bit.' They returned to his bedside and bent over him. 'Come on Joe, you must be feeling better now. Surely you can do better than this.' But these words were not heard and when Sister rang her bell later that evening, the Robinsons left the ward deep in thought. Something was definitely very wrong. And when they passed the other beds of smiling children with their contented parents, they somehow felt alone. As if they were the only couple in the hospital with a really sick child. And yet hadn't Sister told them time and time again 'Not to worry'. Returning home on the crowded evening bus, Margaret and Peter were scarcely aware of the other passengers so deeply were they lost in those very private thoughts. 'What if he were to . . .' but the sentence was never finished nor could they ever share it with one another for fear of arousing quite groundless fears. 'Mickleforth Terrace', yelled the bus conductor. The Robinsons tumbled blindly from the bus. Greetings from their homeward bound neighbours fell on deaf ears. Meanwhile back at home John and Clare anxiously awaited them, demanding all their attention. Only at a very late hour did they finally get to bed.

A troubled sleep for the Robinsons was broken at 5 a.m. the following morning by the front door bell. It's call was urgent and summoned an unwilling, still half asleep Peter Robinson to the door. 'Whoever could it be at this hour? Perhaps there was trouble at the pit.' The door was opened. 'Sorry to disturb you Sir,' stammered a young police officer, 'but we have had a call from Greenhill District Hospital. They're worried about your lad and have asked us to take you there as soon as possible.' 'Oh my God, what if. . . .' Peter checked himself, thanked the officer, and hurried upstairs to dress. This was not the time for a lengthy conversation! 'Don't worry too much dear', he assured Margaret. 'You stay here and care for the children. I'll be back soon.' In a minute he was gone. Mickleforth Terrace was still asleep. Orange neon lights were reflected in the wet asphalt. The roads were silent. The police officer non-committal and Peter afraid.

Within minutes, he was in the hospital. The children's ward was ablaze with lights. The officer followed him discretely, almost as if he were afraid. 'Oh my God, what if Joe's . . . What could I say to Margaret?' As if caught up in a panic and yet trying so hard to conceal it, Peter swept into Sister's office. 'Would you mind waiting in here just a moment Mr Robinson, doctor wishes to come and have a word with you!' Her face was pale, but expression-less. 'Of course he would have a cup of tea. There was no need to ask him.' Without a word she disappeared into the ward kitchen. Peter was alone. The ward staff seemed pre-occupied. Simultaneously, Sister re-appeared carrying the inevitable cup of tea followed closely by the doctor. Neither said a word! The doctor looked tired, as if he had spent most of the night working on the ward. And he played nervously with his stethoscope. Peter felt cold. 'I'm afraid Mr Robinson,' the doctor began his eyes avoiding Peter's searching look, 'I'm afraid I've got bad news for you.' Peter felt lightheaded and he grasped the sides of his chair. 'For God's sake why didn't he come out with it.' 'It's your lad Joe, I'm afraid he died very suddenly half an hour ago. There was nothing we could do for him. I am so very sorry. We did all that . . .' but Peter didn't hear the rest of his words. 'Joe dead!' 'His son dead!' The bright lights of the Sister's office seemed to blind him. Joe's life flashed through his mind. Conception, birth, baptism, first birthday, fifth birthday, eleventh birthday and then the scholarship to St John's. But these momentary visions were swept aside by the flood of tears which now streamed down Peter's face. Suddenly he found a cup of tea in his hand. 'Come on Mr Robinson, drink this it will do you good.' But he wanted no tea. He wanted his son Joe, and alive! Peter cannot remember clearly what happened next. The doctor disappeared without another word. But he can remember Sister squeezing his hand as he left the ward. Then there was the journey home by police car. It was already light and the milkman's float was already half way up the Terrace. He remembers his wife opening the door, her open arms and the tears. The nightmare had begun. The Robinsons had gone into quarantine!

A PROFOUND SILENCE

'A darkness fell over the whole land'—Matt. 27. 45

ALTHOUGH it was still early morning, the news from Green-hill District Hospital was spreading across the Terrace like the ripples in a pond. The house lights came on. Curtains moved. Pale, sleepy faces appeared at windows and peered in the direction of No 22. 'Have you heard the terrible news about young Joe', whispered a neighbour to another as she took in the morning milk. 'He died in hospital early this morning. I saw Peter Robinson return home. You should have seen his face, poor lad!' Horror spread over her neighbour's face. 'Joe! Dead!' And she hurried indoors to hide her tears. What sad breakfast time news she would have for the family this morning. And she didn't know what her boy Andrew would do when he heard the news.

One by one the lights of Mickleforth Terrace came on. Children stirred. Bacon sizzled. People whispered. Within a very short time the ripples had reached the end of the street and a profound silence, the sort of silence which accompanies a November fog, descended upon the whole community. There was no laughter or chatter that morning, and even the paper-boy forgot to whistle as the news reached home. 'Joe dead.' His mate. 'God, what would the gang say?' He hurried home determined to be the first at school (for the first time ever) with the news. Breakfast was a silent affair that morning and as the children, satchels slung over backs, made their way down the

Terrace towards the school bus they hurried past No 22—eyes fixed to the ground for fear of something they might see or hear. They were not quite sure what! Perhaps it was the fear of seeing Joe's Mum, or the fear of being reminded of those happy days spent in knocking a football up and down the Terrace with Joe. Whatever it was they were scared, and their fear only found relief in a burst of nervous laughter as they piled on top of one another into the well-worn school bus. Another day had begun. This would be an opportunity to forget.

Back in the Terrace it was a busy morning and the activity at No 22 did not pass by unnoticed. From behind discretely drawn front room curtains, the neighbours watched the arrival of the family doctor, the local minister and the first relatives. At least one of the neighbours thought she had caught a glimpse of a pale face, that of Margaret Robinson looking from a bedroom window. But she was not quite sure. . . . And how pale Peter Robinson looked, they thought to themselves as he hurried from the house. 'Expect he's going to make the arrangements', remarked one of them. There was no sound of movement from No 22. Clare and John had been taken to the home of a neighbour. They would be well cared for until things had been sorted out. The family doctor had been, but what could he say? He was so close to tears himself that his visit was a brief one. Having prescribed a sedative for Margaret, he momentarily put his arm around her shoulder. Of course he understood, but what could he say. No words could describe his feelings so he left with an assurance that he would return to see both of them again later that day. As for the minister, well of course he knew the family vaguely. As he entered the house, he recalled that he had baptised all the children. Indeed only twelve months previously, their youngest, little Clare, had almost brought the proceedings at the font to an abrupt conclusion by struggling from his grasp. But they rarely attended church and with a parish of about 15,000 people which he attempted to manage single-handed, he really couldn't be expected to know them as well as he might hope. Margaret can remember little of the minister's first visit to No 22. But she thought he said, 'Time is a great healer' or something rather like that, she couldn't be sure. But she did remember him saying, 'Well, perhaps it's a blessing in disguise. After all, he was in no real pain and when the end came he didn't know anything about it.' Yes, she would always remember those words. Words which she found so cruel! Anyway he had only stayed for a very few minutes. Margaret was thankful for that. On that over-cast September morning life seemed to stop for the Robinsons. Their usual appetites disappeared. What was the use of eating? And Margaret, as if in a dream, drifted from room to room in search of something or somebody. She wasn't quite sure what! But then she wasn't quite sure of anything any more. It was as if she were some distant spectator of some great tragedy. A tragedy that could never befall her. Not Margaret Robinson! Yet how her arms ached with emptiness! It was all so quiet everywhere and that morning the usual invitation to go next door to No 23 for the 'elevenses' was not forthcoming. From behind her net curtains she watched her neighbours scurrying to and fro on the other side of the Terrace. At the far end of the street several of them had gathered and in hushed tones they exchanged the sad news. 'Yes, it was true. Young Joe Robinson had died early that morning in Greenhill Hospital. How terrible! And Mrs Folwell had undertaken to collect for the street wreath.' Others hurried passed No 22 casting anxious glances towards the curtained windows. Secretly they hoped they would not see either of the Robinsons, for what could they say? And yet, they just had to look! Margaret thought their behaviour strange

that morning. Instead of exchanging their usual pleasan-
tries with one another, they hurried as if on urgent missions
pre-occupied with secret thoughts. They were all so busy.
'So busy avoiding me', thought Margaret.

Apart from the arrival of relatives, there were no other
callers to No 22 on that first day. It was as if the plague had
visited the household and in terror the community shrank
back for fear of infection. Occasionally an unseen hand
quietly slipped a letter of sympathy beneath the door. 'Dear
Margaret and Peter, We wish you to know how sorry we
are to hear of your tragic . . .', but Margaret could read no
further. It was all so quiet. Margaret longed to go to her
front door and to cry out Joe's name aloud. It was her Joe.
Somebody must care. Surely somebody would come to her
door and let her share her sorrow. But nobody came.
Nobody could! Meals were cooked but scarcely touched
and when the evening sun cast it's long shadows down the
Terrace and the gang returned from school the silence was
complete. No ball bounced across the Terrace that evening.
No marbles rattled in cemented back-yards. Night came,
and with it sleep and escape. Escape from the reality of the
sadness which filled so many homes in Mickleforth Terrace.

And so the days passed. Margaret slept an uneasy,
sedated sleep which knew no distinction between night and
day. It was a nightmare! Peter busied himself with the
'arrangements'. He was never still, always searching for
something to do. Something that would keep his mind if
not his heart away from Joe and the hospital. Further down
the street Mrs. Folwell at No 18 was collecting for the
wreath. 'It would be nice,' she thought to herself, 'if the
whole street would contribute and then we could buy a
big cross of white chrysants and red roses. That would look
nice.' She proceeded to knock on another door. 'I'm
collecting for Joe's . . .' without another word she was
ushered inside with hushed tones. Only when the door had

been firmly closed did they exchange the Terrace news. 'Yes, it was going to be on Friday. The service would be at 10 a.m. followed by interment at Greenhill Cemetery. How Margaret and Peter are going to get through the day, I just don't know! Money changed hands. The door opened and closed. Mrs Folwell made for another house with her news and her purse.

Meanwhile, a few miles away at the College of which Joe had been so proud, the daily after-school informal staff-meeting was taking place. 'As Joe's form-master, Mr Grimshaw, no doubt you'll be attending the lad's funeral on Friday morning. . . . And by the way, it might be a good idea if you re-arranged the seating of the whole class, so as not to remind the other boys of Joe's empty place.'

Friday dawned cold and grey. Even the clatter of the roundsman's float seemed muffled against the chattering of September's first starlings. Mickleforth Terrace was awake. Today they were going to bury Joe. Margaret and Peter had spent a sleepless night, and with the arrival of that day neither of them felt that they had the strength to carry them through. But the gentle, sorrow-worn hands of their relatives coaxed them to stir and to dress. Down in the kitchen a hot drink awaited them. As for the 'gang', none of them went to school that morning. After all, their excuse was a good one and they stayed behind with their parents to watch the arrival of numerous black clad relatives at No 22. 'It's amazing just how many people you can get into one small house,' thought Mrs Smithson as she sipped a second up of tea and, from the safety of her net curtains, watched yet another couple—flowers in hand—disappear inside the Robinsons' house.

At 9.30 a.m. a small deputation from the Terrace, carrying a Cross of white flowers, made its way slowly to the Robinsons' front door. Their progress was followed from a hundred windows up and down the street. They felt important, but how they hoped that neither Margaret nor Peter would answer the door. 'What could they say to them?' Their secret prayer was answered. 'It's for Joe,' they said, 'from all of us in the Terrace.' A relative took the wreath from them and quietly closed the door. Within a few minutes, the hearse appeared at the top of the street. It moved silently, as if wishing to deny the reality of the drama taking place, and slid quietly to a halt outside No 22 amid a gentle shower of already falling petals. The Terrace held it's breath. Necks craned. The 'gang' watched, eyes riveted on the coffin and all those flowers. And now the front door was opening. Curtains moved and faces pressed against windows. 'Yes, it was Margaret and Peter', their faces distorted with grief and sorrow as they slipped into the car behind the hearse. 'Poor thing', muttered a neighbour as she glimpsed Margaret's pale face. As silently as it had arrived, the cortege moved down the street on its journey to the cemetery. Neighbours stood awkwardly at their front doors as the sad procession passed by. Many of them couldn't bear to look, and within a minute the cars had disappeared with no trace of the drama remaining save a trail of flower petals.

Neither Margaret nor Peter can remember the service in any detail. The cemetry chapel was cold and poorly furnished. The carpet was threadbare. The minister appeared in a hurry. He knew the service by heart. Words poured out, but they conveyed very little. Indeed it was only at the committal of Joe's coffin to the grave, that Margaret and Peter suddenly realised the irreparable nature of their loss. They wept un-ashamedly. In a moment it was all over, and anxious relatives were coaxing them away from the graveside to the waiting car. Back at No 22 neighbours were busily engaged. There were plates of ham rolls, finely cut sandwiches and pots of hot tea. Enough for everyone! Curtains were drawn back. It was as if the Terrace had heaved a great sigh of relief. The ordeal was over. Now perhaps they could get on with living!

The Robinsons were not hungry. This was no time for ham rolls and family gossip. Both Margaret and Peter wanted only one thing. Sleep and more sleep! For with sleep the pain of grief was eased, even though momentarily, and it held promise of a sleep from which they would not . . .! 'It's a funny thing,' Maragaret said to herself as she climbed the stairs, 'nobody mentioned Joe's name today, not even the minister. I suppose they're scared. They don't want to hurt me or remind me. But if only they knew.' As the couple disappeared upstairs, the oppressive silence which surrounded the mourners broke into a nervous chatter. A wave of relief swept over them. 'Thank God, they've gone upstairs,' thought one person. At last he could talk in a normal tone and exchange the family news without feeling just a little guilt. And only when Margaret and Peter were well out of sight, was Joe's name mentioned.

How they needed that sleep! And with their waking came a new day. The house was silent. Relatives and friends had gone home and only Margaret's parents had remained behind to keep house for just a few more days. Peter decided that he must return to work and soon . . . if only to forget. And as for Margaret she knew that no matter how she felt, John and Clare were pining for her. She must bring them home today. With considerable effort they dragged on their clothes and made their way downstairs. Outside the gang were already on their way to school. But this morning there was no friendly knock to collect Joe—only distant footsteps echoing in the silence. Margaret could have screamed, instead she bit her lip and bowed her head. There was no breakfast that morning, and even the sight of the familiar tea pot brewed by loving hands made Margaret and Peter feel sick. Within minutes Peter hurried off to work in a desperate bid to forget the horror of the past few days. As he made for the factory bus, people whom he had known for years such as old Bert Henstock from the Greenhill Angling Club—looked the other way. They looked anywhere but at him, seeking to avoid that appeal for help and understanding which they knew would be written on his face. Suddenly, life long friends became speechless; even the bus driver, an old friend of the Robinsons, seemed intent on avoiding his eyes. The bell rang. The bus moved off and Peter sat alone with his thoughts. As for the seat next to him . . . well, it remained vacant for many weeks to come!

Back in the Terrace, Margaret set out to collect John and Clare. It was a sunny morning. The sort of morning which drew the Mickleforth women to their doorsteps to exchange gossip and pass the time of day. This morning, however, the street was deserted. None of the neighbours were to be seen, but from behind windows festooned with thick Victorian lace they watched Margaret as they had watched her child's hearse. What could they say? There was nothing to be said! No words were adequate. Silence was the only answer. Time was a great healer. If Joe's name was never mentioned, she would find it easier to forget! The sun was warm on Margaret's face as she made her way to the end of the Terrace. She was puzzled. 'How strange not a person in sight. They must have heard about our Joe by now. Wasn't he the most popular boy in the street?' Surely somebody would come out to share her sorrow. In the silence Margaret felt she could have screamed Joe's name from the house tops. But what was the use!

Her arrival at No 38 had been anticipated. John and Clare were already dressed and waiting. Their temporary guardian, an old friend of the family, was uneasy. What could she say to Margaret? She would have given anything to avoid looking into the face upon which grief was so clearly written. With a smile, and a comment on their good behaviour, John and Clare were ushered to the door. Once again she smiled. The door closed. Margaret felt that she had been shut out. As she returned home with the children, she secretly hoped that at least somebody from the Terrace would pop their head around the kitchen door for a talk. Somebody who understood how she felt and would let her do the talking!

How long that first day seemed and how silent the house. She moved from room to room. Joe's new school cap, his football shirt and socks drying over the Aga in the kitchen. His place at table. His bedroom door. Everywhere she turned she saw Joe. All the time it was Joe! Blinded by tears she rushed to the door . . . perhaps it was all a dream. Yes, of course that was it! It was all a bad dream from which she would soon be awaking.

But this was a dream which had no end. The firm but gentle hand of her mother upon her shoulder reminded her that there were jobs still to be done. The children had to be fed and now they needed her love more than ever before.

Only Margaret and Peter Robinson can tell us just how much they suffered at the hands of the community of Mickleforth Terrace during those days and weeks which followed their son's funeral. Suddenly, almost over-night, they found themselves completely alone. Joe's death had transformed the character of the Terrace. Mrs Smith, who had at one time been such a good friend of the family and was always asking anxiously after the welfare of the children, now rarely came to the house. She always avoided doorstep confrontations with Margaret. Indeed, Margaret suspected that she was avoiding her purposely. And when one evening the gang passed by on their way back from school they ignored her and just went on whistling and kicking a pebble before them as if she had not been there. How Margaret longed to talk about Joe—but how they feared her tears! Or were they frightened of their own? Occasionally Margaret met one of her friends who was prepared to stop for just a moment—but when she did, her neighbour as if to avoid any mention of Joe, talked about everything under the sun. 'It's going to be a cold winter, they say,' she remarked, 'and some say there'll be a lot of snow.' But Margaret was not really listening. Why all this talk about the weather? She wanted to talk about the person upper-most in her mind—Joe!

Peter found it no easier at work. His boss had told his work-mates, 'Carry on as if nothing has happened. For God's sake don't mention it. You'll only upset him.' On the contrary, Peter longed to talk about his son. About his successes at school. How he longed for that opportunity. An opportunity denied him because his colleagues felt that 'it's all water under the bridge now. There's nothing that can be done, so why let him wallow in his own grief?' On the bus to and from work, every street corner, every group of boys reminded him of Joe. His Joe. But nobody would let him talk about his dead son.

The days were no easier with their passing. Margaret's mother went home. The golden days of Autumn vanished as the gloom of November approached. Rain lashed the windows and a choir of broken gutters sang their lament. John and Clare demanded all their mother's attention, but they seldom received it. 'If only I hadn't scolded him and turned my back on him when he needed me most. Oh God, why did it have to happen to us? We've never hurt anybody', thought Margaret.

The Coroner's verdict of 'Accidental Death' brought her no comfort. 'Why us?' But what was the use? Life still had to go on. The house had to be cleaned and the food cooked. Everything seemed to require twice as much effort as before. Before it happened, Margaret's day in the home had been broken into at regular intervals by the arrival of a friend from down the Terrace. It may have been half a pound of cooking fat, a packet of cigarettes or even the proverbial cup of tea, but whatever it was, they had always come to Margaret.

Things had changed. Now they never came, or if they did they never had the time to step inside. Sometimes, Margaret felt she could bear it no longer and with tears streaming down her face she would go around to No 21. 'Now come on my dear', her neighbour would remark. 'You've got to shake yourself out of this mood and try to forget all about it. It just can't be helped. Besides, you've got two other lovely children and a husband to care for. They need your love more than ever now.' There her help ended. On some afternoons, Margaret would try and rest with the children. How she longed to sleep and go on sleeping. Perhaps, perhaps she would never wake up! Wasn't this what she really wanted—to go to sleep and never wake up? Margaret was appalled at those thoughts and she wondered if Peter had ever felt the same. Of course, she had never seriously considered suicide, but sometimes . . . and then she changed her thoughts.

But if only she could share this thing with Peter! Of course, he had been good to her—nobody could deny that. But he seemed unwilling to discuss Joe, and whenever she mentioned his name he became angry—told her 'to pull herself together' and then changed the subject. How he had changed in so short a time, she thought. 'He's not the same man I married.' Nor indeed was he! Coming from a pit home in the Rhondda, Peter was well acquainted with death and disaster. He remembered how as a boy he had stood with his father at the pit head and watched them bringing up the bodies one by one. He had seen death before. Of course he longed to talk about his lad, just like

31

any other father. But tears were not for men and he knew that Margaret would understand. He must try to make her forget the past, and in doing so he hoped that he might be able to forget it himself.

Days, weeks and months passed. Joe's name was never mentioned now, Margaret and Peter Robinson unable to share their grief with one another went their separate ways. Housework, and the care of John and Clare, absorbed an increasing amount of Margaret's time, and Peter, well, he seemed to be spending more and more time away from home. Of course, the overtime was always needed at No 22, but some of the neighbours were already beginning to talk . . .! Margaret had her suspicions too. With the passage of time their love, which had been founded on their mutual love of Joe, grew cold and in it's cooling the conspiracy of silence grew.

3

THE GREAT UNMENTIONABLE

> My grief is still as keen as ever, mainly
> because no-one has ever let me talk about
> it, not even a minister or doctor.
>
> Bereaved mother

THE innocent victims of a conspiracy of silence, Margaret and Peter Robinson suddenly found themselves placed in quarantine. Their son's death had made them contagious. They had become a threat to the emotional stability of the Mickleforth Community and, as the Old Testament leper had been excluded from the life of his village until such time as he was pronounced clean by the priest, so the Robinsons found themselves deprived of community care. They were enshrouded in a conspiracy of silence, at the heart of which was that great unmentionable—Death!

Contemporary society's inability to accept the reality of death and its corporate denial of any real help to the bereaved continues to produce an ever increasing number of casualties like Margaret and Peter. And yet there can be no doubt that the crisis of bereavement is one of the oldest emotional problems with which mankind has had to contend. It is perhaps true to say that death, like few other subjects, has exercised the minds of most of the world's greatest philosophers. No other subject has attracted greater attention in the world of poetry, nor received so much time in debating chambers and forums. To understand the reasons why Margaret and Peter have become victims of this contemporary taboo, we should look at the change in our attitude to death and bereavement over a period of some three hundred years.

Two thousand years before the birth of Jesus Christ, the Psalmist wrote: 'The days of man are but as grass, for he flourisheth as a flower of the field. For as soon as the wind goeth over it, it is gone and the place thereof shall know it no more'. It is not surprising that these words from Psalm 103 have found their way into the Liturgical office for the Burial of the Dead. Their usage reflects an age of sanity when death was faced as a reality—when the pastoral care of the bereaved was a community responsibility.

Three hundred years ago, England's strength lay within her village communities. Life was short and often ended violently. Because of its brevity, life was taken seriously and the care of both the living and the dying was a corporate responsibility. From the cradle to the grave, the cycle of man's life was the concern of his neighbour. It was as a community that the whole village rejoiced at the birth of the squire's son and heir, and when the old man died they carried his body to the grave, tolled the bell and shed their tears. Death was no stranger! The plague was a not infrequent visitor, and many an English graveyard records in stone and brass the sorrow of Tudor mothers many times bereft of their children. Justice was harsh. Many a wayside gibbet and city gate bore grim testimony to those who broke the law. No, death was no stranger to these homes—for those who worked England's soil and watched the swine foraging for acorns beneath the eternal oaks had seen it all before. A thousand times. Spring, summer, autumn, winter—their lives had been moulded by the passage of these seasons and, as spring always followed winter, so their faith assured them that death was not the end, only the beginning. Among these people death was no enemy!

But in three hundred years much has changed. Vast impersonal conurbations have replaced and silenced for ever the traditional pattern of community care. Man, we are told, has come of age. Decimal currency jingles in his pocket and the keys to success are a fast car, a holiday abroad and a colour TV. The village midwife, the family doctor and the parish priest are fast being replaced by an impersonal system of codes and groupings. With developments in medical research, the average expectation of life has been almost doubled and the personal ministry of the local herbalist with his prescriptions for blackberry leaves and nettle tea has been forgotten in the wake which spells progress. The age of the Welfare State has arrived and all is well. After all, man's journey from the cradle to the grave is covered by a series of grants!

Despite all the progress made in the many different spheres of life, loneliness has become one of the greatest scourges of our age. Whole communities have been swept away and vast blocks of flats have been filled with uprooted people. Loneliness, frustration and boredom have often been the fruits of progress.

Many of us believe that we are self-sufficient. We have no need of our neighbour's help and *they* don't need *us*. That may well be our attitude until we realize that forty-five per cent of all hospital beds are occupied by men and women suffering from mental disorders because of their inability to cope with the stresses and strains of contemporary living; that over thirty million working days were lost in 1967/1968 through mental illness; that each year 4,500 people kill themselves in the United Kingdom, many of them because of the isolation into which society places them through no fault of their own, and that another 40,000 people make an unsuccessful bid to end their lives. Could this cry for help be made any louder? Meanwhile there are 400,000 alcoholics in this country and several million of us regularly take tranquillising or anti-depressant drugs prescribed to relieve some of the mental and emotional strain which confront us daily. And of course, there is a growing prison population of some 33,000 men, women and young people.

Need more be said. The fact that all is not well, despite the security of a Welfare State, has not escaped the notice of an increasing number of far-sighted and compassionate people. From the concern for the special needs of important minority groups, whether suffering from alcoholism or bereavement, have emerged many voluntary organisations (Coventry, for example, has 300) all seeking to help individuals in a variety of circumstances. In their wake, local councils of social services have been formed, thereby co-ordinating the work of both statutory and voluntary organisations and bringing a considerable amount of relief to a great number of people.

But contemporary society's understanding of the human life-cycle, and the crisis of death and bereavement, has to be examined in the context of an age which is post-Christian—as well as in the context of a fragmented society. Only a tiny minority of Britain's population nowadays profess to be practising Christians of any denomination. Although public opinion surveys have disclosed that outside this minority there are quite a number of people who have some almost undefinable belief in life after death, a belief no longer related by them to Christianity, it would seem that for the majority of people in these islands the Christian Church and the Gospel it seeks to proclaim can have little relevance to their lives. This is the age in which Man has conquered space. The stars and stripes fly on the moon—a witness to man's courage, his determination and his scientific skill. It is the age of human heart transplants when pioneers such as Christian Barnard have brought new life to condemned men. They have smiled and turned their

36

backs on death. Seemingly, it is an age which knows no limit to man's determination to hang on to life. Man is a proud animal. All that he possesses—his home, his car, his status within society—are the fruit of his hard work. We are told that an 'Englishman's home is his castle' and so it is. All that he holds most precious lies within it's walls, and in his wife and children, his glory is reflected. For such a man, his world, his castle is a secure place. Indeed he is the master of his destiny, or so he believes. The world is his home. Bloodshed in Northern Ireland and Vietnam; a flood disaster in the Ganges Delta and the picture of a half starved and half dead refugee on the front of his morning newspaper—all seem rather remote, rather distant from his life and his way of living. Even an Aberfan or a local airline disaster fail to shake his confidence in himself.

It is in this context that the crisis of death and bereavement assumes a superficial if not unrealistic character. For men such as these, there is no room for death on their itinerary of life. Life is far too full, far too exciting ever to find time to contemplate that obscenity—death! For how many men can objectively contemplate their state of non-being? Death has become an obscene word in a society which regards this crisis as an unspoken threat to all that they possess. A threat to all that they hold most dear. Death has become that great 'unmentionable' enemy to their peace of mind. If this is the case, then we must ask ourselves what becomes of man when he is suddenly confronted with this crisis. A death in the home or an unexpected death in the office can have tremendous repercussions within the traditional framework of community life, but what effect does it have, if any, upon today's fragmented society? Does the death of a close relative or friend shake man's self-confidence? Does he begin, perhaps for the first time in his life, to re-examine those values on which his life and the lives of those whom he loves are based? Does a personal bereavement in the life of such a man result in his adoption of a completely new approach to the whole question of life and death?

The answer to all these questions is to be found, I believe, in the massive corporate denial of the reality and significance of death which is so destructive in the life of contemporary society. Man evades the issue of his mortality. In Britain, and in many other countries, death is taboo and has become a dirty word in an age which believes itself to be immortal. Indeed, some undertakers aid and abet this unhealthy conspiracy by making corpses look as if they are still alive and so encourage a dangerous way of escapism for the bereaved.

The reality of death and it's finality is denied by many, and the bereaved are alienated in the midst of life. Modern man, like the Levite in the parable of the Good Samaritan, passes by on the other side of the street. In silence! Although he may deny the fact, there can be little doubt that death in close proximity will have disturbed him considerably. After the initial shock however, like the Spartans on the battlefield, he will link arms in a show of bravado with the remaining members of the community and carry on as if nothing has happened . . . always making sure, of course, that the quarantining of the person who has actually suffered the bereavement is still effective.

Traditionally, the Levitic and priestly communities or castes had nothing to do with the Samaritans. As with the leper who was excluded from the life of the community until pronounced 'clean' by the priest, so the Samaritan found himself classed as one of the 'untouchables' of his day . . . beyond the reach of even his neighbour's help when he lay dying on some street corner. This enforced exile, whether of a temporary or permanent nature, by a community of special 'classes' of individuals is vividly recorded in several places in the Old Testament—but none so movingly as in the Book of Job 19. 13, 14:

> My brothers stand aloof from me,
> and my relations take care to avoid me.
> My kindred and friends have all gone away,
> and the guests in my house have forgotten me.

With these haunting words, the anonymous Hebrew author of the book of Job describes the isolation and devastating loneliness into which the central character of his story was driven by the community as a result of a seemingly unending succession of personal disasters. The story records how Job, a rich and happy man, and a faithful servant of God, is put to the test by his Creator. The narrator describes how Job loses all his possessions. His children are killed in a violent storm and, as if that isn't enough, his own person is attacked by a plague of malignant ulcers which cover him from head to toe. His sickness is revolting and painful. His grief almost unbearable. Almost overnight, as the direct result of his misfortune, Job finds himself a social outcast and alienated from that society of which he is a son. Financial disaster, bereavement, sickness—all these personal tragedies were used by his family and his friends as an excuse to place him into quarantine, as an excuse for his temporary exile. And they needed these as excuses because they had no idea how to cope with Job's emotional trauma.

How do you cope, when a person whom you know to be kind and good suffers not only bankruptcy, but the loss of his children and the loss of his good health? Are words adequate? And if they are not, what other alternative have you than to leave him alone with his problems. This was, I believe, the dilemma facing the relatives and friends of Job. Their inability to help and comfort him, when he needed their help most, could only be solved by his temporary exclusion from any active participation in the life of the community. Out of sight—out of mind . . . it seemed to solve some of their problems and left Job quite alone to face his!

Margaret and Peter Robinson became the innocent victims of a dilemma similar to that of Job's. Quite suddenly, they had lost their most prized possession—their son Joe. Words were not adequate! How does the circle of relatives and friends say 'I'm sorry' in circumstances such as these? How can they share in the reality of Joe's death whilst at the same time seeking desperately to preserve their own peace of mind? How can they be of any real help to Margaret and Peter in enabling them to accept the reality of their loss, when they themselves would rather walk by on the other side of the road. And do so! The Robinsons when left in isolation and loneliness when their son died. The leper was excluded from society because his disease was contagious. He was unclean and, in an age which associated illness with sin, he required the priest's blessing before he could be welcomed back into the community.

Margaret and Peter had been bereaved. In the eyes of the community in which they lived, they had come in contact with something which was contagious—death. Contagious because it had the strength to break their conspiracy of denial and to confront them with the awful facts of their mortality. To avoid such an encounter, and all the repercussions that would follow, there was a need for the carriers of the infection to be isolated. To be placed into quarantine until such time as their emotional trauma had been purged and they were no longer considered a threat to the community. All this happened to Margaret and Peter! Not only did they lose their son in death, but in many ways far more grievous was their treatment at the hands of people who they called relatives and friends. People from whom they had every right to expect a special depth of understanding and help. But then of course, these expectations were based on the false assumption that the people who lived in the Terrace were capable of dealing with such a crisis in their midst. After all, hadn't the Robinsons been members of the same conspiracy before they became victims of it! Apart from the traditional courtesies which such a neighbourhood as Mickleforth would observe, such as the donation of a street wreath, it is most unlikely that Margaret and Peter would have deviated from the common reaction to a sudden bereavement, to the death of somebody else's child and not their own. But then they never thought it could ever happen to them.

It would seem that the mental suffering through which the Robinsons passed after the loss of their son was partly of their own making, and until such time as the Taboo on death is broken this situation will arise again and again. Only when it is realised that the key to the re-habilitation of the recently bereaved lies in the pocket of the community as a whole, will we be able to care adequately for people like Margaret and Peter. We all believe it could never happen to us and when it does, in a very real sense, we are speechless and help is not forthcoming. We stand appalled by death's impertinence. We shut our eyes to its presence and, when it comes, we are confounded.

Our attitude to death, then, has changed as the direct result of living in a post-Christian, fragmented society. Corporate responsibility for the dying and the bereaved has been replaced by an egoism which is concerned only with the survival of the fittest. Those who are bereaved, suddenly find themselves sent into a bewildering exile from which few emerge mentally unscathed. The taboo on death can only be broken when the conspiracy of silence which surrounds it has been dispelled, and realities faced. Meanwhile, we have to ask ourselves what is to become of the bereaved? A nation's attitude will not change over-night, nor will society willingly undertake to share the grief of others if this grief is a threat to their own peace of mind. To whom then does the bereaved person turn in his darkest hour? The Church? His neighbours? His family doctor? The health visitor, or perhaps to that uneasy sleep which comes with sedatives and alcohol?

Until the community is re-mobilised to care for the bereaved, the professionals—whether doctors, clergy or health visitors—should closely re-examine their own role in that special ministry to those who mourn. For it is through these men and women and their own awareness of the needs of the bereaved, that the community may take new heart and may once again exercise a real care for those who would otherwise have no reason left for living.

4

REACTIONS TO GRIEF

At this grief, my heart was utterly darkened . . .
I was miserable and without joy.

St Augustine

WITH Joe's death, Margaret and Peter Robinson entered
that strange land of grief through which most of us will one
day have to pass. It was not a unique journey. The path
had been well trodden! Indeed, the cry which burst from
David's lips when he learnt of the death of Absalom echoes
across the years:

'The King shuddered. He went up to the room
over the gate and burst into tears, and weeping
said, "My son Absalom! My son! My son Absalom!
Would I had died in your place! Absalom, my son
my son!" '

2 Sam. 18. 33 J.B.

There are always two parties to a death; the person who
dies and the survivors who are bereaved. As Arnold
Toynbee reminds us in *Man's Concern with Death*, 'The
capital fact about the relation between living and dying is
that there are two parties to the suffering that death
inflicts; and in the apportionment of this suffering, the
survivor takes the brunt.' The sentiment expressed by
David in his grief and sorrow is a universal one. How
many times Margaret and Peter had secretly wished that
they could have taken Joe's place. 'If only . . . if only!'

43

But would they not have wanted to spare him the suffering which they themselves were undergoing? Would they have willingly wished upon him the pain of bereavement? I do not think so!

Grief is a reaction to the loss of an object of love and, as such, is not confined solely to human beings. There can be little doubt that a lioness suddenly deprived of even one of her cubs experiences a sense of loss—though this may be difficult to measure. But even human grief is a complex process because of the complexity and variety of human nature. The psychiatrist may list a succession of phases in the grief 'experience' through which the human has to pass on the road towards re-habilitation after bereavement, but the depth and duration of these phases, as indeed their impact, will vary from individual to individual. The ability to cope with grief depends on yourself, the help you get—and the circumstances.

In the story of Absalom, we are told that David was rebuked by his commander-in-chief for letting the death of his son turn the day of victory into a day of mourning. The death of Absalom must not overcloud the glorious victory won. The King and his court were still alive! To mourn on such a day was a shameful thing. Following a strict military code, David is encouraged to bury his grief. The people's good becomes before personal sorrow—as so many great statesmen have had to learn since. Of course, David was never quite the same again and it is doubtful if his grief was ever really resolved satisfactorily. In this story there are similarities to that of Margaret and Peter.

It is important for the community to care for the bereaved, and such care will only be forthcoming when grief is viewed objectively. The people who lived alongside the Robinsons in Mickleforth Terrace had experienced grief subjectively time and time again! Two World Wars, pit accidents and malignant disease had taken it's toll.

The personal experiences of bereavement had been so painful that they wanted to forget—not become involved. Most of us try to forget the pain of bereavement as quickly as possible. We try to spare ourselves further agony! Perhaps this is the reason, or one of them, why the neighbours in the Terrace felt themselves unable to help Margaret and Peter. They were afraid of being hurt again. They feared that if they went to the young couple's help, old wounds would be re-opened . . . their wounds.

It is true, of course, that only the Robinsons could do the real work of grieving for Joe, because Joe was their lad and nobody else's. Only their own tears and their own agony would bring them healing and wholeness. The tears of others wouldn't help.

The people who lived in the Terrace knew this as they shuffled silently—like David's army returning from their victory—to the very edge of the crisis area. As spectators, a crude word perhaps, they would not be hurt nor could they hurt . . . or so they thought. Somehow, they just didn't understand that Margaret and Peter desperately needed the company of somebody to share their sorrow. Somebody whose friendship would keep them rooted to reality at a time when sorrow and grief tempted them to the brink of insanity.

It may help us to understand grief a little better: if we examine some normal and abnormal reactions which we may expect to find in a person who has recently been bereaved. We must remember that the following study, although based on Margaret and Peter Robinson's loss of Joe, is bound to be inadequate as each individual is a unique personality and so will differ in his reaction to personal bereavement. Again, the nature of the grief experienced will vary according to the circumstances which surround the death of the person mourned—as indeed the depth of grief and it's intensity will depend on the closeness of the relationship between the deceased and the survivor.

According to Lindemann 'acute grief is a definite syndrome with psychological and somatic symptomatology'[1]; for this reason I shall divide the grief reaction into normal and abnormal and then into physical and psychological.

NORMAL REACTIONS

PHYSICAL SYMPTOMS

(a) *Shock and Numbness* Although it happened quite some time ago, both Margaret and Peter can recall in vivid detail the moment when the news of Joe's death was broken to them. It was a moment of disbelief and unreality. Both can remember, and will always remember, the face of the person who first broke the news to them. They knew what was being said but their inner mind could not register the words. 'Joe is dead.' Of course there were tears, but suddenly both felt as if they were in a dream world. It was not happening to them. It was happening to somebody else, not to the Robinsons. And even when the 'in-laws' arrived to help arrange the funeral—somehow they seemed remote and distant. When Margaret and Peter discussed the service with the vicar, they secretly did not believe it was happening to them. It must be a nightmare! And yet Joe's grandmother was wearing black. . . .

(b) *Sleeplessness, Loss of Appetite, General Apathy* The pain is still there, but Margaret has learnt to smile again. She recalls that when she heard of Joe's death she lost her appetite almost over-night. Food made her feel sick and within a month she had lost almost two stone. 'My clothes

[1]Symptomatology and Management of Acute Grief, E. Lindemann (*American Journal of Psychiatry* Vol. 101, No 2, September 1944).

46

hung on me like the rags on a scare-crow', she remarked. She had never known such long nights. They seemed interminable, and the monotony of the alarm clock's tick was frequently broken by excursions to the kitchen for a pot of tea. But the tea was never drunk. Half empty cups littered the bedroom as well as the kitchen. And then there was that long wait for dawn. It could never come too quickly for Margaret and Peter, and yet when it did arrive they felt unable to face the day.

Peter was just the same. He knew he had lost weight because he had been able to pull in his belt an extra four notches . . . something he had not been able to do for a long time! No amount of persuasion could make him eat any of his regular meals, and when relatives coaxed him to watch his favourite TV programme he found he wasn't really watching it. His mind was miles away . . . with his Joe!

There were days, the Robinsons will recall, when they could not set their minds to even the smallest task. Letters were left half-written, chores around the house went unfinished. The place looked dirty, and yet somehow they just hadn't got the energy to get on with it. It was too much like hard work. On other days they found themselves lost in a frenzy of activity. They were so busy forgetting or at least trying to forget . . . trying to forget the reality of their loss.

And then, quite suddenly, they would realise that there was no going back. It was not a dream. Joe was really dead! The tears would flow unceasingly. Their bodies would ache with emptiness as if nature's kind anaesthetic was suddenly disappearing to reveal the true horror of the wound they had sustained. Margaret had never known such pain before. She recalled that when Joe had been born a mixture of gas and air had eased him into her arms, but now it was as if her womb was wretching for the boychild it had borne. How she longed for an end to it all. For an end to the pain, for an end to the nightmare, for an end to . . . and then the sleeping pills would bring a brief respite as she fell into a drug induced sleep. To surrender anything of oneself is always a heart-breaking experience and to give up one's child—that was the cruellest thing of all:

'Oh Absalom, my son, my son!'

Yet Margaret knew that when she could accept the fact of surrender and loss, then only would peace of mind come.

Of these most painful days in her life Margaret seldom speaks. She is trying to forget the past, but she knows that she never will and, very secretly, she never wishes to!

PSYCHOLOGICAL SYMPTOMS

(a) *Guilt* Margaret will never cease to blame herself for speaking as she says, 'unkindly' to Joe whilst he lay in the children's ward of Greenhill District Hospital. Her sleepless nights (and many of them still are) were pre-occupied with self-reproach. She never meant to be unkind. She was just tired and worried and the words slipped out. She didn't mean them! But how would Joe ever know that? At night, she often wondered what Joe must have thought of her when she was so abrupt with him. She imagined that he was upset, that he may have cried when she left the ward. 'Oh my God, why, why, why?' Of course, the family doctor pointed out to Margaret that she was in no way to blame for Joe's death. But then, in her heart of hearts, she knew this already and yet somehow she still wanted to blame herself!

Peter had no such problem. He knew that he had done everything possible to help his lad. No father could have done more! And as for Margaret, well what more could he say to remove that feeling of guilt? Nothing!

(*b*) *Hostility* Why had Joe died? Yes, of course she knew the answer which the Coroner had given to her. She knew it by heart but that didn't make it any easier. Why did her Joe have to die when he had so much to live for? Had she done something wrong for which God was punishing her? Perhaps it was because many years ago she had ... but why Joe and not her? But if she wasn't to blame, who was? It was the surgeon! That was it! It was the surgeon who operated on Joe and brought the virus into the operating theatre. He was responsible for the lad's death. She would have legal redress! She would accuse him of criminal negligence! She would sue him for every penny that he possessed and have his name erased from the register of the Royal College of Surgeons. That's what she'd do!

But hadn't the Coroner returned a verdict of 'Accidental Death'? There was no question of criminal proceedings! She could of course obtain further legal advice and seek redress through the civil courts. Oh God, why did it have to happen? Why did you take my Joe? Why?

(*c*) *Idealisation* Of course, Joe had always been their very special boy. They knew he would do well! Hadn't the Junior School always said he would? There was not another boy like him in the Terrace! Always well-mannered, good at school and on the soccer field. He had so many winning ways! Margaret found it increasingly difficult to remember the real Joe ... the mud caked soccer shirt and shorts on the bathroom floor week in and week out ... the number of times she had told him not to leave them upstairs but to put them in a bucket in the scullery! And then of course, along with the other members of the gang, he knew his bit of cheek!

No, Joe Robinson had not been a 'perfect' lad. Nor had his father wanted him that way. But Margaret preferred to remember none of this. He was her boy and not even the two other children would be quite as wonderful as him!

(*d*) *Identification with the Deceased* In the months following Joe's death, Margaret became increasingly pre-occupied with her memories of Joe as he used to be. Somehow she felt that her memories of him would keep him alive for her. She recalled that he had had the habit of placing the knives the wrong way around when he could be bribed to lay the table. One day, quite unconsciously, she found that she had done the same. She smiled. Joe wasn't quite so far away as she had thought. And anyway, Peter never noticed such things!

(*e*) *Pre-occupation with the Deceased's Image* How the Robinsons longed to hold on to their son. It was the parting, the accepting of the reality of their loss, which was so painful and yet at the same time so important to their recovery. Wherever they went, they harboured that secret hope that they might step out of their nightmare and find themselves face to face . . . with Joe! Time and time again when they were out shopping, one or other of them would think that they had caught a glimpse of Joe disappearing into the crowd or crossing a road. On one occasion, although she could never tell Peter, Margaret had actually run down a street after a boy who was the 'splitting image' of her Joe. She called out his name again and again and again, but he went on his way ignoring her. How she ran! But when she touched his shoulder and he turned to face her . . . he was nothing like Joe! What a fool she had felt as she apologised to the boy and retraced her steps.

Of course, Peter had seen his lad a thousand times. Wherever he saw a group of boys playing football he saw Joe in their midst, and on more than one occasion he had checked himself only just in time from calling out a greeting to him. He was glad that Margaret hadn't been with him.

But then of course he knew that his imagination was playing tricks. Joe was dead and there was nothing more to be said—or was there?

How long the journey back to 'normality' takes is a matter of dispute among the specialists. Freud suggested six months, whereas Lindemann thought that after six weeks the bereaved should be showing signs of recovery.[1] Marris, however, found evidence of grief persisting for two years after the death of a wife. It is obvious that there is no fixed time because of the wide variance from person to person. Many people are still grieving two or three years after bereavement. The Robinsons are just such a family, and where the symptoms are prolonged we should ask if the grief is normal or abnormal.

ABNORMAL REACTIONS

Psychiatrists suggest that abnormal reactions to grief are the result of an exaggeration and or prolongation of those symptoms which were experienced by Margaret and Peter. It would seem that they occur when grief has been either postponed or delayed at the time when the death occurred.

Lindemann classified the abnormal grief reactions as follows:

1. Over-activity without a sense of loss. The sub-conscious denies the reality of the loss incurred. The bereaved person throws himself into activities of an expansive and adventurous nature.
2. The acquisition of symptoms belonging to the last illness of the deceased. It is not uncommon for those recently bereaved to experience the pain and discomfort which were characteristic of the deceased's last illness. Sometimes they occur at the time of an anniversary. The

[1]See Peter Marris' *Widows and their Families* (Routledge and Kegan Paul, 1958).

prolongation of such symptoms may result in the sufferer being labelled either an hysteric or an hypochondriac.

3. A recognised medical disease, namely a group of psychosomatic conditions, predominantly ulcerative colitis, rheumatoid arthritis and asthma.

4. Alteration in relationship to friends and relatives. Sometimes the bereaved person gives up all social contact and lives the life of a recluse.

5. Conduct resembling schizophrenic pictures. These people seem to go about in a continuous daze, behaving in a formal or mechanical way and avoiding all emotional expression.

6. Furious hostility against specific persons. As in Margaret's case the doctor is accused of neglect and proceedings are often threatened although rarely carried out.

7. A complete lack of initiative or drive. The bereaved finds it extremely difficult to make decisions or to complete any course of action without the help of relatives or friends.

8. Behaviour which is not in accord with his normal social and economic existence.

9. Severe depression with insomnia, feelings of unworthiness, great tension, bitter self-reproach and a need for punishment.

These sombre abnormal reactions to grief point to the very real dangers which exist if men and women are denied the opportunity of coming to terms with their loss. If contemporary society's whole attitude towards death and bereavement inhibits the adequate expression of grief then we may well expect that an increasing number of those recently bereaved will require psychiatric advice and help in the years to come.

But in our study of the reactions to grief, we must

remember that grief and pain is the price we humans have to pay for the love and total commitment which we have for another person. The more we love; the more we are hurt when we lose the object of our love. But if we are honest with ourselves, would we have it any other way? Would Margaret and Peter have wanted it any other way?

When we give our love to another person we give part of ourselves, and in our love we become one with them. When we lose their physical presence through death we lose part of ourselves. It is as if we have suffered a real amputation. If you lose a limb then you receive very special care from the medical authorities during the period of rehabilitation. Both your physical and mental health are the concern of a great number of people. You will not be discharged from care until such time as they are really quite sure that you are able to cope.

There is no need to draw further parallels between the needs of those recently bereaved and those who have recently undergone an amputation. We would not dream of leaving the amputee alone. Surely the Margaret and Peter Robinsons of this world have every right to expect similar care and thought on our part.

Grief only becomes a tolerable and creative experience when love enables it to be shared with somebody who really understands.

5

THE BEREAVED AND THE CARING TEAM

What is wanted is a compassionate listener who
will let them talk about their loss from every
aspect and be prepared to let them cry and to
cry with them.

A Bereaved Mother

PETER ROBINSON will never forget that early morning drive
to Greenhill District Hospital. The neon lights, the nervous
young police officer, the ward sister with sorrow and defeat
written across her face, and his son Joe—seemingly so small
and white upon his hospital bed. Nor would he forget a
second visit to the hospital later that morning, when an
embarassed doctor surrounded by silent nurses handed
him a buff envelope containing the death certificate. Joe's
death certificate. This time he travelled home alone in a
taxi.

But what of the hospital staff? What was to become of
them now that Joe was dead? Of course, there were other
patients in the ward all needing love and care. Indeed,
Joe's bed was already in use again, but somehow things
were not quite the same. Nobody would deny the fact that
the whole ward team had worked desperately hard to
save the young boy's life. Nothing had been spared in the
attempt to save him. But to no avail! Joe had died and
more than one nurse had been found shedding frustrated
tears that morning. But the life of the ward could not stop.
There were too many mouths to feed and dressings to

change. The doctor went back to his rounds, but without a smile, and sister found her junior nurses not quite as efficient as they usually were. She knew why! The Joe Robinson file in it's smart green jacket was closed. His name indicator was removed from the bed's head. His locker emptied and his possessions—"the gang's football shirt," and his wristwatch were bundled into a brown paper sack to await his father's collection.

Later that morning, sister watched silently as Peter Robinson left the hospital in a taxi. Beneath one arm was that brown paper sack and, crumpled in his left raincoat pocket, was the death certificate. The hospital had done all that it could possibly do. Now its was up to the community to care for Peter Robinson and his wife. But as the taxi swung out of the hospital drive, sister wondered, as she always did after a death in her ward, what would become of the bereaved parents. Would people really understand how they were feeling and would they ever get over their loss? Somehow she felt that the Robinsons were going to have a tough time ahead of them . . . but then the telephone brought her thoughts back to the ward. 'This is Casualty Department, sister, we're sending up a twelve year old girl with multiple injuries received in an RTA. She's unconscious.' Sister sighed and left her office.

The ward sister's anxiety about the after-care of Margaret and Peter Robinson was well founded. It would seem clear that the hospital's care of the next of kin really ends when the death certificate is signed. The file on the deceased is then closed. The bereaved family return home to find that things have changed. Of course they're in a state of shock which initially numbs their senses. They can't believe it has really happened. . . . But something else less tangible has changed as well. Neighbours look the other way. They walk on the other side of the street. They talk about every other subject. But not about. . . . From the intensive care of the hospital ward, they are sent home to a community which does not want to know them.

There are flowers. There are letters, but seldom a compassionate listener who will let them talk about their loss and be prepared to let them cry and to cry with them. Tears are an outrage to their decency. Tearful people must be avoided. Suddenly the bereaved find themselves alone in a strange new world. A world in which they are apparently left alone with their grief. If they are unable to receive help, either from the hospital or the community, then we should ask ourselves two questions: (1) Is there a valid ministry to the bereaved and of what does it consist? (2) Who is responsible for exercising this special ministry?

Margaret and Peter Robinson are evidence enough that there is a need for a valid ministry to the bereaved. This ministry should follow the general principles of any ministry to those in crisis. This includes the provision of material aid, comfort and moral support. Those who exercise this ministry—and we shall discuss who they are to be later—have the important task of encouraging the mourner to face the reality of his loss. Whereas friends and neighbours, to avoid a confrontation with the reality of death, encourage those bereaved to forget the past and to carry on as if nothing has happened, those who are really concerned to see that the bereaved *work through their grief* will encourage them to face the reality of the situation. This is always a painful process. To accept the fact that a person who you love is dead means that you must surrender that last very secret hope that it's all a bad dream from which you will eventually awake! To part with such a dream, and to acknowledge that death has taken place, means that you can then give yourself to the important but unpleasant task of grieving.

A Lincolnshire mother writes that 'for months after our son's death, I felt a physical pain such as I should imagine having an arm or leg amputated must feel. How my arms ached with emptiness.' Few of us would volunteer for such an experience, and perhaps this is what persuades many of our neighbours to become involved in this conspiracy of silence.

Those who would help the bereaved through their grief must be prepared and willing to enter to some degree into the other person's experience, while controlling the depth of his own emotional involvement. Unlike close relatives and friends whose main aim is 'to distract and cheer', the person who befriends the mourner must establish a close enough relationship to enable him to talk freely and at length about his grief and sorrow. To discourage an obviously distraught person from sharing his grief, and to attempt to 'change the conversation' can have disastrous consequences. The bereaved never cease to be amazed by the lack of support from those who knew them well. A bereaved father writes, 'My wife found difficulty in obtaining support from a surprising number of relatives and friends, she having to protect them from the reality of our loss, so as to avoid upsetting them.'

For many mourners, such as Margaret and Peter Robinson, the 'Valley of the Shadow' through which they pass after bereavement is a place which thankfully has no comparison on earth. If walked alone with no guide, no strong shoulder on which to lean, it assumes all the characteristics of a terrible nightmare from which one never wakes up. One mother described this period in her life as 'passing through hell', whilst another wrote, 'To us his parents it has been a heart breaking journey through strange country of very often faltering faith in God and humanity.' A third, writing from Northern Ireland, said, 'I felt like a leper in those first weeks, though I realised my neighbours only avoided me because they couldn't cope with the situation. They did not know what to say.'

During the critical phase of bereavement grief requires as much expert handling as an unexploded bomb. If the community cannot handle the situation, then specialists must be called. But the supportive role of either community or specialist cannot be restricted to any specific period after the actual loss. Many mourners discover that it takes months, sometimes years, to re-adjust to their bereavement and that throughout this time there must always be a person to whom they can turn to share their frustration and sorrow. The bereaved are frequently hurt when impatient relatives or friends tell them to 'snap out of it'. The maxim that 'time is the greatest healer' does not look always quite so convincing. A Yorkshire mother writes, 'It is thirty-four years since our eldest child died and I do not think there is a waking hour when she is not in my thoughts. Not even one's nearest friends want to talk about it and this is one of the worst parts to bear.'

Perhaps we have established two facts with which we might begin to answer the second question. Firstly, that the sharing of personal grief with a person who really understands our sorrow is of important therapeutic value. A trouble shared is a trouble halved! But because of the conspiracy of silence which surrounds death, many people are denied this opportunity of sharing and so their path towards rehabilitation is impeded. Secondly, if the community finds itself unable to care for the bereaved members in it's midst, then surely some other body must make this special ministry their responsibility. For far too long medical authorities have assumed that the Peter Robinsons of our day were being adequately cared for by their neighbours, and for far too long the society in which we live has made the false assumption that all is well in the field of community relations . . . that is until somebody dies!

If this is the case, then the time has arrived for us to

have a serious look at the question of who is responsible for exercising a special ministry to the bereaved? Ideally this is a community responsibility, but as we have already seen in the history of Margaret and Peter, the community very often fails the bereaved. In this context, it would seem that there is a need for some professional body not only to dispel the conspiracy which surrounds death but also to mobilize the community so that adequate provision is made for such people. Meanwhile, perhaps we can best answer the question of responsibility by examining the roles of those people through whose hands the Robinsons passed throughout Joe's stay in Greenhill District Hospital—and after his death. If we can assess where their responsibilities within the crisis situation lie, then we shall be able to begin to formulate a procedure for the after-care of the bereaved. This study, as it affected the bereaved couple, can be drawn up under five headings: the hospital, next of kin, the family doctor, the parish priest or minister, the health visitor.

(1) *The Hospital* From the outset of the drama, the hospital's team of specialists were involved. The diagnosis was appendicitis and nobody anticipated complications. The admission clerk, the ward sister and the senior houseman had seen it all before and they prepared for a routine appendicectomy. Nor was such an admission a new experience to junior members of the nursing staff working on the ward. Initially, their first priority was the removal of Joe's troublesome appendix followed by post-operative care. And both of these tasks were performed successfully. At no time was there any reason to suspect that the outcome of the operation would be fatal. And when the sudden relapse did come, nothing was spared in the attempt to save the young boy's life. But when that battle was lost and the death certificate signed, the hospital

closed it's file on Joe Robinson. It had done all that it could possibly do, or so it thought.

The greatest weakness in the ward system where Joe had been a patient was the lack of communication between members of the caring team. Although ample provision could have been made, at no time during the ward's weekly timetable was half an hour set aside for members of the medical and nursing staff to meet together to discuss the tensions and anxieties which arise quite naturally in the ward's crisis situation. Of course, the patients and their needs were never far from their thoughts and they had frequently been talked about in the nurses' dining room, but they never sat down as a team to talk through some of those problems which arise from the ward's daily life. The doctors and nurses were highly and selectively trained in the science of saving life, removing pain and arresting the spread of disease, but nowhere in their training curriculum was mention made of the importance of their pastoral ministry, should the patient not get better! At no time during their training did either profession who cared for Joe receive a lecture in the pastoral care of the bereaved. Joe, because he was ill, was their responsibility alone. It was never thought possible that the patient might die and that his dependents might become—if only for a very short time—their responsibility as well!

But then Joe did die! And neither doctor nor ward sister ministered adequately to his parents. For two very good reasons they failed Margaret and Peter Robinson when they needed their help most. The first reason may be said to be applicable to society generally. Neither doctor nor sister had worked out their own personal philosophy of life and death. Neither had made room in their private time-table to face the inevitable fact of non-being. And it is difficult to be of any real help to the bereaved until you have realistically faced your own dying.

Greenhill District Hospital was one of our few modern hospitals. No expense had been spared to furnish it with the best equipment, but when a person died within it's walls it found itself powerless! Apart from a highly equipped mortuary and a brown cardboard box of shrouds hidden away in the linen cupboard of each ward, no other provision was made for the dead and those who mourned their passing. When Joe died, neither doctor nor sister could offer any further help. Their task was over, and in the privacy of their own rooms they would have to work alone through their own frustration and grief. Perhaps, if they had the opportunity to share this grief with other members of the staff in a weekly ward conference, they might have been better equipped to meet such an emergency should it arise again. A cup of tea and a guiding hand at the taxi door will not alone resolve the problems of grief!

Secondly, the hospital failed the Robinsons because it had given insufficient thought to the after-care of the bereaved. They had never asked themselves what became of distressed relatives when they left hospital. Where did they go? Who cared for them? As we have seen, they just assumed that they would step back into their place in the community. The ward sister who had witnessed Peter Robinson's final departure from the hospital with his son's death certificate had felt uneasy. She did wonder what was going to become of the couple, but then her attention was distracted and she gave no further thought to the matter. 'Surely somebody was going to care for them'; she thought to herself. But of course, nobody felt able to help them and we already know the rest of the story!

This failing must not be attributed solely to the hospital's lack of fore-thought in it's care of the bereaved. It would seem that neither medical social worker nor hospital chaplain commended the care of the Robinsons to their counter-parts in the community. Had the medical social worker alerted the local mental health officer and the health visitor who served the Mickleforth area, then it is quite possible that Margaret and Peter would have been spared a considerable amount of unnecessary suffering. They would have been helped in facing the reality of Joe's death at a much earlier stage.

This assumption that the mental health officer and health visitor would have been of real help to the couple is based on the hope that both of these specialists would have already come to terms with their own dying, and would have worked out their own philsophy of life and death. Some hospitals make adequate provision for the after-care of the bereaved. But this was not so in the case of Greenhill District Hospital and, because there was this serious omission in an otherwise highly commendable organisation, it is all the more important that every hospital should have a blue-print for the commendation of the bereaved to the care of the community.

Several important questions are raised by Joe's death— questions which every hospital must look at very carefully.

(a) Is adequate provision made for a weekly ward conference to enable members of both the medical and nursing staff to discuss at some depth the emotional crises which do arise in the ward from day to day?

(b) Is a lecture on the pastoral care of the bereaved included in the Training School syllabus?

(c) If 'death' is an obscene word in hospital, then surely a day's conference held in the Post-graduate Medical Centre on this very subject would produce considerable feedback and benefit in the life of the hospital!

(d) What provisions does a ward sister make for the care of bereaved relatives when they leave her ward?

(e) In the event of a death on the ward, who is responsible for notifying the parish priest or minister, the family doctor, the health visitor and, possibly, the mental health officer?

If these questions are answered, then there is no doubt that realistic action will be taken to prevent a similar occurrence in the hospitals which have no system for dealing with the bereaved. Of course, members of both the medical and nursing staff work under very considerable pressure most of the time and it is important not to add to the demands made upon them. However, until such time as the hospital can be quite sure that the bereaved are not going to be alienated from the community because of their contact with death, they must make quite sure that the specialists in the community are involved from the outset in this special work of caring. Ideally, when a death takes place on a ward, the sister should be responsible for informing the 'next of kin' *and* for mobilising the other specialists.

Greenhill District Hospital, however, had worked out no such plan for helping the bereaved. They were unable to help Peter and Margaret. They passed the problem back to the Robinson family and left them to get on with it! So in the early hours of the morning, with his silent companion, Peter Robinson returned to the Terrace and to his next of kin. He and his wife had every right to expect *their* support at least, but, as with Job, 'my relations take care to avoid me. My kindred and friends have all gone away'. Peter and Margaret found themselves isolated by their family.

(2) *Relatives and Friends* The Robinsons' relatives and friends were shocked and embarassed by the boy's sudden death. Suddenly death and the experience of bereavement had come very close to them and they feared it's proximity. Of course, as soon as they received word of the tragedy, they travelled from all parts of the country to be with Margaret and Peter. Within twenty-four hours of Joe's death, all the

family had arrived. Parents and grandparents, doting uncles and aunts. They filled the house to capacity, but their shallow laughter and idle chatter scarcely concealed their own sorrow and distress. Somehow they thought that this was no time for tears—no time for reminiscing. They must be brave for the couple's sake. They must show no sign of human weakness! No tear must betray their feelings!

How Margaret and Peter resented this play acting . . . this acting a part! How they longed to weep and pour out their hearts in the company of people, who should after all understand how they feel! But all this help was denied them, and they found themselves supporting their relatives in this crisis—rather than their relatives supporting them. We have already heard how close Margaret was to screaming when they talked about every other subject under the sun rather than mention Joe's name. They just couldn't wait for the funeral to be over and for an excuse to leave the house and to forget . . . To forget that death is just around the corner!

Between Joe's death and burial the house was filled with relatives, but few if any of them were of any real help to Margaret and Peter whose initial heartbreak was numbed by a state of shock. The real pain was still to come. The last wreaths were layed and the ham sandwiches had disappeared. Now, for the very first time, the couple were almost alone. Just when they needed help most, as the reality of their son's death burst through that initial state of numbness and shock, the relatives kissed them 'Good-bye' and went on their separate ways.

'Relatives forget and think that one week is long enough to get over your loss' wrote one bereaved mother. She continued, 'Please help us. We so often hear people advising us to pull ourselves together . . . but no-one has given us any helpful suggestions.' The Robinsons had every right to hope that those who knew them best would be the ones who would help them the most. Those who had watched them grow up from childhood and had followed their courtship with special interest. Those who had attended their wedding and were godparents at Joe's baptism—these were the people upon whom Margaret and Peter had relied for help during a crisis of this sort. But once again, this help was not really forthcoming because neither their relatives nor friends were able to help themselves. And how could they help this young couple, when they were fighting inwardly all the time against the reality of such a terrible thing as the death of a young boy. A boy called Joe.

What *is* the role of relatives and friends in this particular crisis situation? How can they help the process which leads towards the acceptance of loss and social rehabilitation? As has been said earlier, the ministry to the bereaved should follow the general principles of a ministry to those in crisis. Provision must be made for strong moral support of the bereaved—sustained over a period of several months —whilst the bereaved person works through this period of grieving. A week in 'that' house was long enough for most of the Robinsons' friends and relatives, but when they left after the funeral Margaret and Peter had not even begun the work of grieving. The only people who know the strengths and weaknesses of any particular family are the friends and relatives of that family, and they alone are best qualified to help and carry the family through the experience of bereavement. Only he who knows the depths of relationships, which are the strength of every family, is able to understand fully the implications when a member of that family dies. How the deceased person spoke, his mannerisms, his interests in life, his failings and his successes, these are all of vital importance to the bereaved as they relive their life with that person during the first phase of real grief.

So many friends and relatives when confronted with this

crisis within their own family circle tend to encourage a way of escapism for the bereaved. The deceased person's name is never mentioned, not only because it is synonymous with the word 'death', but because to preserve their own conspiracy of denial, they would encourage the bereaved to forget the past—as if it had never had happened. This denial brings them peace of mind . . . but for how long! The needs of the bereaved are summed up in these words by a bereaved mother: 'What is wanted is a *compassionate listener* who will let you talk about your loss from every angle. This is something I miss among my relatives and friends. However sympathetic they may be, their main aim is to distract and cheer me. How can you be expected to cut off from your thoughts and conversation someone who has formed fifty per cent of your thoughts almost from the day of conception?'

To be a compassionate listener, then, is the role of relatives and friends in this particular crisis situation. They must forget self and encourage the bereaved to talk at length and in detail about their loss. There will be tears and long silences. They will hear the life history of the deceased person and the intimate details of his or her death bed over and over again. The compassionate listener need say very little, for his interested presence at the side of the mourner is far more important than anything that he can say. Just to be there and listening to what the mourner has to say is a major contribution to that person's social re-habilitation. It is no easy task! Sometimes it is very painful and distressing. The danger of uncontrolled emotional involvement is always close by, and yet this is the most positive form of help which the family can offer. Didn't St Paul admonish the Romans 'To weep with them that weep!' (Rom 12.15). Once the funeral is over and the flowers are dead, the greatest need that for the compassionate listener is just beginning.

There can be no doubt that, had sensitive relatives and friends become the much sought-after compassionate listeners in the lives of Margaret and Peter when their Joe died, then possibly their loss could have been the means whereby that taboo on death in the Mickleforth community was destroyed.

Peter returned from the hospital. The news was broken to Margaret. There were tears. The family was informed and the family doctor arrived—with him came his sedatives and his tranquillisers. What is his role within the specialist team?

(3) *The Family Doctor* Called by a well-meaning neighbour to No 22 who thought that he might be able to help, the doctor found himself speechless. What could he say? He had been caring for the Robinson family for almost ten years. He had watched young Joe grow up from a babe in arms. He had watched him playing football down the street. He had helped to deliver Clare in the local hospital and he had arranged for Joe's admission to the Greenhill District Hospital. All he could do was to prescribe a sedation for Margaret and momentarily put his arms around her shoulder. He would be seeing her again! There was little else he could do. He prescribed sedatives, but these would only delay the beginning of the real work of grieving. And some time that had to be faced! To 'blot out' grief by taking several sleeping tablets would only delay that crucial initial step of accepting the reality of one's loss— that vital step towards wholeness of body and mind.

Like the medical staff at the District Hospital, the Robinsons' doctor had received no formal training in the pastoral care of the bereaved during his days as a medical student. The clinical nature of death had been widely discussed, but never it's repercussions in the context of the family circle and society generally. At no time after his admission to hospital was there any communication between Joe's doctor and the house surgeon. And when Joe died it was not the hospital who informed his family doctor as a precautionary measure, but an anxious neighbour!

It should have been the responsibility of a member of the medical or nursing staff to inform the family doctor, who then in turn would be in a position to mobilise statutory bodies to help him in the care of Margaret and Peter. With his medical skill and knowledge of the family, the doctor becomes the ideal compassionate listener— although from the point of view of time available he might well contest this suggestion! But he is a key figure in the care of the bereaved. It is true of course that the role of the family doctor is changing. With the exception of his ministry in rural communities, where the doctor is still very much a friend of the family, the general practitioner in urban areas finds himself working under tremendous pressure with a responsibility for the well-being of several thousand people. Under circumstances like these it is difficult for the doctor to take a personal interest in every bereaved person on his patient's list, but at least if he has knowledge of their need and their sorrow then he is in a position to enlist the support of other specialists, so that at least somebody can 'look after them'.

(4) *The Parish Priest or Minister* 'I have never met my parish priest. I think he has about 30,000 parishioners up here'— so wrote a bereaved mother living in Belfast, Northern Ireland. Margaret and Peter were not practising Christians. They had had Clare baptised at the parish church only twelve months ago, but this was really only to pacify rather irate and, as they thought, rather unimaginative grand-parents. They had gone through with the ceremony, but found it rather a bore and rather embarrassing. As indeed did the Vicar!

68

They remembered that he arrived at almost the same time as their doctor. They had wondered if their doctor went to Church. . . . But then they didn't really understand what the Vicar was saying to them. Perhaps that was because they could only think of Joe. They wanted to talk about their Joe, but the parish priest was more intent on talking to them! And so little of any importance was said. He had of course been gentle with them . . . assuring them of his prayers and another visit to finalise the arrangements for the funeral. But of all the people who had been to visit them since their Joe died, he seemed to be the most pre-occupied. He was determined to say his piece and then he hurried off. In his care were 15,000 souls and he worked the parish single-handed.

Like that parish priest in Belfast, he worked alone. His congregation was small but they were deeply committed to Christ and his Church. As he hurried away from No 22 he realised that there was a desperate need to mobilise the Church to care for people such as Margaret and Peter. He knew that he would find it difficult to visit them regularly after Joe's funeral, and yet he knew that if he could find somebody in his congregation who perhaps had experienced a similar loss, then perhaps they could make a weekly call on the household. 'It's a good idea', he thought to himself, but then his mind moved to another matter.

The ward sister was well experienced in caring for patients of all denominations. She prided herself on having met priests and ministers of every religion and denomination. If the patients were registered as 'RC' then she never hesistated to inform the part-time Catholic chaplain that there were patients on her ward requiring his ministry. As for those registered as 'C of E', she was never quite sure who to contact and when. She knew the hospital's Anglican chaplain, but so many of her patients registered themselves as 'C of E' thats he was never quite sure whether to call a priest to them or not. She didn't wish to offend anybody.

Joe was a 'C of E' according to her file. The night they had fought so hard to save his life, she had been in two minds as to whether to call in the Anglican chaplain or not. But then things happened so quickly and it was too late! And when Joe died the file was closed, and she never thought to commend the Robinsons to their own local parish priest because she assumed that he would already know about their plight. Once again Greenhill District Hospital closed the file on the dangerous assumption that somebody would provide adequate pastoral care for the family living at No 22.

Again, it has to be underlined that the cleric is a member of the specialist team and together with the family doctor must share the responsibility of enabling the bereaved to face the reality of their loss. By virtue of his vocation he is also the most suitable person to mobilise the Christians in his care to their corporate responsibility for the welfare of those people recently bereaved. Had he mobilised those members of his congregation who live in the area of Mickleforth Terrace to care for Margaret and Peter, by providing them with some compassionate and patient listeners, then much unhappiness would have been avoided. In the sphere of bereavement, it is the Church's responsibility not only to preach the Gospel of the Resurrection, but also to share the burden and the heartbreak of those bereaved. This is not an easy ministry and demands much of those who seek to lighten the grief of others. As the Archbishop of Canterbury reminds us, 'In your service of others you will feel, you will care, you will be hurt, you will have your heart broken. And it is doubtful if any of us can do anything at all until we have been very much hurt, and until our hearts have been very much broken.'

But this is the risk which the Christian Church must be

prepared to take if she is to care adequately for those who mourn. In an age which denies the reality of death and the existence of God, we must break this taboo. We must, by word and by example, demonstrate that, far from being a negative experience, grief *can* become a positive source for good in the lives of those people whom it visits.

(5) *The Health Visitor* She had heard of the Robinsons. News of the tragedy had not only hit the headlines of the local newspaper, but in every house that she had visited Joe's name was the main topic of conversation. 'Had she been asked to visit No 22? Did she know that Margaret and Peter Robinson were going through a very bad time? Had she heard the rumour that the family were going to leave the district?' The health visitor remained silent. She knew that if her services were required then she would be called. Her wait was not long.

The day after the funeral the family doctor called again on the Robinsons, as he did on several occasions during the first six months after Joe's death. There was little he could say to ease Margaret's grief, but perhaps the local health visitor might provide her with an opportunity to talk and her needs could be assessed. The health visitor found Margaret on the verge of a nervous breakdown. Marital relationships were under strain. Perhaps, if a relative could care for the other children, she might be able to persuade the Robinsons to go away together for a little while to sort out themselves. She wasn't encouraging them to escape from the reality of the situation, but she did feel that they needed a little privacy to talk about the future. She knew just the place where they could go. And if they wanted her advice, well they knew her telephone number. So with skill and tact, the local health visitor, and other members of the specialist team, averted another tragedy at No 22.

What have we learned from the experience of Margaret and Peter Robinson, and can it benefit the community as a whole:

(1) That the conspiracy of silence which surrounds death has pervaded the whole of contemporary society.

(2) That every individual has a responsibility both to himself and society to work out his own philosophy of life and death.

(3) That such an exercise should be included in the training curriculum of every doctor, nurse, social worker and parish priest or minister. Only when these professions have come to terms with their own dying can they hope to be of any real help to those recently bereaved.

(4) That every hospital should commend the bereaved to specialist care in the community. When a death occurs in hospital a member of that specialist team should automatically inform not just the next of kin, but also the family doctor and the parish priest.

(5) That these two specialists should in turn mobilise the neighbourhood, and both statutory and voluntary bodies to care for the grieving family.

(6) That whilst the privacy and wishes of the mourner must always be respected, their greatest need is for the compassionate listener who must find the time and the courage to share their grief and heart-break.

(7) That the experience of bereavement and of loss can become a destructive force in the lives of the bereaved unless there is somebody alongside them who can help them to channel it.

In the next chapter we shall look at the history and work of one of the voluntary organisations which has emerged, quite spontaneously, in answer to *crie de coeur*. It was to such an organisation as the Society of the Compassionate Friends, that the Robinsons' family doctor and parish priest turned for help. For the care of the bereaved is both an individual and a corporate responsibility.

6

A MINISTRY OF COMPASSION

The greatest shock is that one does not expect
one's child to die before oneself.
A Bereaved Father

EVERY year, 27,000 homes in Great Britain mourn the
death of a child. Margaret and Peter Robinson lived in
one of these homes. Many of these children die on our
roads, whilst others fall victims to such malignant diseases
as cancer. The children receive every possible medical and
nursing care. Nothing is spared in the battle for survival.
And nobody feels the sense of defeat and failure when a
child dies more than the medical and nursing staff.

But what of their parents? They become victims of a
society in which the word death is forbidden. They are
denied the opportunity to accept the reality of their loss
and to work through their grief. This denial produces
neurotic and unrealistic responses in many of the parents,
and the tragic consequences may be far-reaching. Under
the special conditions of stress, the whole system of com-
munications in the home may break down, and in some
cases the marital relationship of the bereaved may be
damaged irreparably. In these circumstances, which are
often very traumatic, the remaining children manifest an
increasing variety of symptons which point to emotional
instability and stress. Furthermore, unresolved grief may
well result in the onset of mental illness requiring specialist
treatment of either one or both parents, and even of the
children, for an unspecified period.

It was an awareness of the size and complexity of this problem of parental grief which, in January 1969, prompted a group of bereaved parents living in the City of Coventry to form a society to offer help and understanding to those bereft of their children. The society was called the Society of the Compassionate Friends and, one year later, it became a national organisation with branches in many parts of the country. To understand the reasons which prompted the formation of this society, and why it grew so rapidly, we need to go to the childrens ward of another hospital.

In May 1968, two young boys lay dying in a Midlands hospital. Billy was twelve years old and was suffering from cancer, an illness which had been diagnosed some twelve months previously. Kenneth, who was eleven years old, had sustained serious head injuries when he had been knocked off his bicycle on his way to school. During the vigil which the boy's parents kept in the hospital at the bedsides of their sons, they got to know the assistant hospital chaplain. Although they never actually met until after the boys had died, the chaplain became the link between their separate needs.

The sun shone. The Precinct was a mass of cherry blossom, and the blue sky promised a beautiful summer. Peacefully, within a few days of one another, Billy and Kenneth died. Shortly afterwards the boys' parents met for the first time. Immediately a warm freindship developed, which, based as it was on a mutual understanding of the sorrow and heartbreak which had accompanied their own personal tragedies, was of tremendous therapeutic value to both families.

A year passed. The chaplain met the two families frequently and walked alongside them through that strange valley of grief. Meanwhile another one hundred and eighty children died in Coventry! As this friendship developed, this small group of people began to realise that in the sharing of their grief they had found hope and courage, and they had not given away to despair. Without fear of embarassment, and in the context of a deep understanding of each other's bereavement, they wept unashamedly—with those tears came healing and wholeness. They talked of their boys—of their likes and dislikes and when so moved, the tears flowed quite freely and unhindered; with them came a new faith in life and in the future.

But what of the others? How could the comfort and healing which they had discovered among themselves be shared with so many thousands of other bereaved parents in desperate need? How could such a tiny group of people lost in the untidy sprawl of a great industrial city bring friendship, understanding and hope to thousands of men and women who had lost children?

Before we answer these questions, let us look more closely at 'the others'. Those bereaved parents, like the Robinsons of Mickleforth Terrace, who through their loss found themselves alienated from society and quite alone. These were the people about whom the Coventry group were so concerned.

'Please, please help us! We do not know how we can face Christmas this year. We feel so desolate and alone. Can you help us? What can we do?'

'The house seems so lonely and quiet. I seem in a daze most of the time with little interest in anything and yet when he was alive I was involved in so many things.'

'My husband thinks it is "best to forget". I have tried to share this thing with him, but he just does not want to know.'

'Oh God, I killed her because I was too tired to test her brakes. The new ones on her bicycle.'

'It was me, I did it. He asked me to go swimming with

76

him and I refused. If I had been with him as he asked, he would never have drowned.'

'Why did God have to take our Rosemary? It was my fault, I let her go out alone. Why didn't he take me instead?'

'We were all so happy! We did everything together and he was so full of life. He was the only light in our lives and now that he is dead neither my wife nor I seem to have any purpose left for living.'

'The curate said that her death was a blessing in disguise. That was of no comfort to me. Even though her brain injuries were extensive, I would have devoted my life to caring for her.'

So wrote men and women from all walks of life who were united by that common bond of suffering, the death of their child. Some were haunted by an element of guilt. Others, finding themselves unable to share their grief with either their spouse or close relatives, were on the verge of a nervous breakdown. Others seemed to have given up the struggle a long time ago. The loss of their only child seemed to damn them in the eyes of the world. They wanted no pity. They just wanted an end to it all. Sweet peace, oblivion! Others asked 'Why?' A thousand times, Why? But there was no answer to their question. Only an embarassed silence as the community went about it's work.

Oh yes, that group of bereaved parents meeting in Coventry knew just how 'the others' felt and they were determined to help them. They were quite determined to meet the need for an active lay ministry in this special field of pastoral care. On the night of 28th January 1969, they met in the Nurses Home of the Coventry and Warwickshire Hospital. At this meeting the Society of the Compassionate Friends was born, and the first six founder member, which included the parents of Billy and Kenneth, placed on record that the Society's aim was. . . .

'To offer friendship and understanding to any person,

irrespective of colour and creed, who finds himself or herself heart broken and socially isolated by the death of a child.'

Because of their own personal experience of this type of grief, and because they had found comfort and healing in it's sharing, these men and women realised that membership of the Society, if it were to be of any use in it's serving 'the others', would have to be restricted to bereaved parents.

The group multiplied as friendships developed from a mutual understanding of each other's tragedy. Meetings were held frequently in each other's homes and no embarassment was shown when a member of the group burst into tears. Each knew how the other felt. Each knew the nature of the other's loss, and in this atmosphere they felt they could be themselves. The mask which society had expected each of them to wear was quickly discarded.

And so, very slowly but in a very real way, healing came. There was no dramatic transformation, no overnight miracle and no sudden personality change. Such changes as these would have provoked only consternation and the cure would have had no great depth. But for those of us who worked alongside these parents, the slow but definite healing process was quite visible. Men and women who had lost all interest in the world around them following their bereavement began to take an interest in life once more. The father who sold his car because he associated all cars with his son's death bought a new one and was encouraged to drive again. A mother, who for almost two years had refused to enter her daughter's bedroom, now pulled back the curtains and threw the windows wide open With their opening, the unmentionable shadow of despair and purposelessness fled the house. She bought a new dress and so she began to live again. These couples, once broken by grief, had been taught by their membership of this group to enjoy life once more without feeling that somehow it was wrong. The photographs and souvenirs which well-thinking relatives and friends secreted away when the child died 'to save his parents from further pain' have now reappeared and occupy their familiar places. And so healing takes place!

Within a short time of it's formation, this small group of bereaved parents had won the confidence and the support, not only of their own family doctors who marvelled at the practical and very realistic way in which they were working through their grief, but also the unqualified support of clergy and ministers of all denominations. Both professions recognised the importance and value of the help which this group was offering to bereaved parents living in the Coventry area. The Society of the Compassionate Friends was offering help to bereaved parents by putting them in touch with those, who, because they had suffered similarly, could share their grief constructively. It's essence was to see that people helped each other and so helped themselves. This was group therapy—and it worked.

A member of the group who had already worked through her own grief undertook the responsibility of recording all parental bereavements within the city boundary. Another wrote a personal letter on the Society's behalf offering understanding friendship to every couple so bereaved. Some weeks later the letter was followed by a bunch of flowers. Not for the grave! Amid the flowers was a small card from the group on which was written an address and telephone number. A compassionate listener would be at the service of the bereaved parents day and night should they need this help. All they had to do was to dial a number!

And so, very slowly, the life of this Coventry group evolved. It's membership grew in number. Those who saw broken people restored to 'wholeness' within the framework of this caring community became a little uneasy about our neglect of 'the others'. In Coventry, at least, a small attempt was being made to tackle the problem of parental grief, and with some success! We all knew this! But who was to care for 'the others'? How could this small group of bereaved parents meeting fortnightly in the Midlands share the secret of their success with thousands of others. How were others coping? To whom did they turn for help in time of despair? The answer to this question was not far away.

In December 1969, when the Coventry group had only been meeting officially for some eleven months, the BBC invited the Society to contribute a short talk to 'Woman's Hour'. The parents of Kenneth spoke quite simply of their loss and of the loneliness which society had imposed upon them in their time of grief and bitterness. And they spoke of the healing and the friendship which membership of this group had brought them. No, they were not indulging in their grief nor was it morbid curiosity! For the very first time they had been able to share their grief fully with people who understood, and in it's sharing they had discovered a sense of freedom, a sense of liberation from the traditional fetters which the contemporary taboo on death places on the bereaved. The recording lasted ten minutes duration.

The talk was broadcast on Friday, 12th December at 3 p.m. The following morning the first letters arrived. They came from the far North of Scotland where a crofter's wife told of her grief and loneliness. They came from Eire and from the sparkling seaside resorts along the Sussex and Kent coast. From the industrial cities of the Midlands and the North of England, letters poured into the Society's office in Coventry describing the heart break and grief of so many. And from villages lost amid the green folds of the West Country came pleas for help and friendship. These were 'the others' about whom the Coventry group had been so concerned. There was a terrific need to be met, and met soon if needless tragedies were to be averted. The parents of Billy and Kenneth now realised that somehow the Society's work would have to be developed on a national scale to meet the needs of hundreds and thousands of men and women whose lives had been shattered by the death of a child.

All the letters were answered personally and with great care. But, as the recipients knew from bitter personal experience, a letter was just not enough. For many of those who had written, the physical presence of a compassionate listener was far more important. Somebody to whom a bereaved parent like Margaret Robinson could have turned in time of depression or despair. Somebody who would understand and who would want to understand. Somebody who would make time to listen. Despite this anxiety, the parents in Coventry felt quite sure that the need would be met . . . and it was! For with those pleas for help came offers from mature men and women who, having worked through their experience of child-loss, felt able and willing to minister to others. Since that broadcast in 1969, the work of the Society of the Compassionate Friends has been extended to many parts of Britain, and today the Society is engaged in the process of developing a chain of self-help groups or branches stretching from Cornwall in the far West through the industrial Midlands to Scotland.

It is now four years since Billy and Kenneth died in that Midlands hospital. Much has happened, and another hundred thousand children have died in these crowded islands. But out of that initial heartbreak and grief a vision has been nurtured. A vision of a society which will become nation-wide in it's care of those who mourn the death of a child. In 1972, that vision is fast becoming a reality. With the support of publicity on both a national and international scale the Society has now extended it's healing work to many parts of the country. It is very likely that, as a result of increasing correspondence from North America, the next two years will see an extension of the Society in the USA and Canada.

Although much has happened since 1968, the people who are intimately associated with the life and work of the Society and the problem it is seeking to tackle, are very conscious of the fact that their ministry in this special field of community care has only just begun. There is still much to learn. In a speech at the second Annual General Meeting of the Society it was said that 'The Society is still only a baby—this evening she is two years old and only just beginning to make her first few hesistant steps towards childhood. Because of this we must always be ready to learn, to hear the view of others and to accept and benefit from their constructive criticism. In time, I am quite sure that this child will reach adulthood.'

Of one thing, however, the Society is already quite sure. That un-resolved parental grief on the scale of which we have seen constitutes a very real threat to the mental health of this small but important minority group. We have learnt, in our attempt to understand the deepest needs of bereaved parents, that every couple reacts very differently to their loss and no two deaths can have quite the same repercussions in the life of the family. For example, the loss of an only child, and the resulting grief in the lives of a middle-aged couple will have very different repercussions to the loss of a ten year old girl who is survived by an elder brother or a younger sister. We can look at the distinctions within parental grief a little more closely.

The Death of the Only Child 'We were all so happy. We did everything together and he was so full of life.' The untimely death of the only child is always a most grievous loss, and it would probably be true to say that few parents, if any, ever fully recover from such a bitter blow. So many of these parents have equated their only child with the future. People can sometimes be heard to say, 'They must be sorry they only had the one child.' Yet if they knew! If they knew that the child had been born after a succession of unsuccessful pregnancies . . . or that it was the long awaited child on an adoption list.

When the only child dies many parents believe for a time that they nothing else to live for. It is not surprising that there is quite a high incidence of mental illness in this category of parental grief.

Sibling Grief What became of John and Clare, the nine year old brother and eighteen month old sister of Joe Robinson? How they had loved their elder brother! And how John aspired to his brother's skill with the football. Then, quite suddenly, Joe died and the two younger children, without any explanation, were secreted away until such time as the funeral was over and they could return home. When they did return to No 22 something had changed. Somehow their mum and dad seemed more aloof and more pre-occupied than usual. And without Joe, things seemed so strange and the house so quiet. They felt forgotten and rather alone.

In the context of the pastoral care of bereaved parents, there is a tendency either to forget or neglect the emotional needs of the surviving children. Frequently, parents may be 'blinded' by their own grief to the needs of their other children. We know that quite often parents become especially attached to one child or another. There seems to be a favourite in every family, and the Robinsons were no exception to this. How they loved their Joe! But then Joe died, and Margaret and Peter were so immersed in their own private grief that they failed to meet adequately the needs of their two surviving children. Had the Robinsons not received some specialist help, there is a strange possibility that they would have idolised Joe to such an extent that their remaining children would have become jealous and resentful. In cases where the dead child has been 'canonised' by his sorrowing parents to the exclusion of the other children, it has been shown that the siblings become anti-social in a desperate bid to attract attention and to win back their parents love.

The faults and weaknesses which beset the child before his death are quickly forgotten, and parents remember only what is good and beautiful. This is a natural reaction, but it does become dangerous, even harmful, when the parents start to compare the 'faultless' child with their remaining children. Instead of finding consolation in their presence, the bereaved parents tend to see only their faults and in some cases the bereaved mother completely rejects her other children. This illness is particularly hurtful to the husband and his children, the latter not understanding their mother's rejection of them. Frequently this difficult phase is terminated by mental illness requiring specialist treatment.

The parish priest and the family doctor must be on the look out for signs of parental rejection of the remaining children, and must be prepared to discuss these deep feelings with those parents involved.

The Element of Guilt How Margaret Robinson reproached herself for not being more patient and understanding with Joe when he lay dying in Greenhill Hospital! Indeed, it is quite probable that secretly she will reproach herself for the rest of her life. That is, of course, unless she is able to share her feeling of guilt with somebody who is able to help and understand her. The element of guilt is a common factor in parental grief. The failure to see a child across a busy main road, to check the brakes on a recently renovated pedal cycle, or to change well-worn car tyres are just as likely to produce a guilt complex because of their disastrous consequences as is the suicide of a teenager. In such circumstances as these, the element of guilt is always destructive and unless resolved in the company of a sympathetic friend may have grave repercussions. Once again the parish priest and family doctor must be alive to such possibilities and ready to enlist the help of other specialists should the situation arise.

Marital Discord 'I have tried to share this thing (her grief) with my husband, but he doesn't want to know.'—this was Margaret Robinson writing to a friend some six months after her son's death. When a home is bereft of a child, the first person to whom the mother automatically turns for comfort and consolation is her husband. In him, even though she may be in a daze, she can find the necessary strength and courage to meet the difficult days ahead. Often, as the result of being plunged together into this sort of crisis situation, husband and wife discover a new depth and strength of love between them which they did not know existed. And despite their loss and it's finality for them, many of these parents do grow closer together. For others, however, things are very different.

The death of the only child, sibling grief, the element of guilt and marital discord are four of the main causes of tension and anxiety which any members of the specialist caring team may encounter when visiting a home mourning the death of a child. Three of these elements were present at No 22 Mickleforth Terrace in the days following Joe's death.

The story of Margaret and Peter Robinson emphasises the importance of the intensive care which every bereaved couple requires from the caring team. This team should include the parish priest, the family doctor, the health visitor, the marriage guidance counsellor and the medical social worker. We are told that 'time heals'. Indeed it does—but the scar always remains.

Sickness, old age and death constitute a challenge which each one of us will one day have to face. But whether we face this challenge alone, or in the company of people who are prepared to share our burden and lighten our grief, depends on our willingness to take this problem seriously.

In 1959, the Cruse Clubs founded by Margaret Torrie began its specialist ministry amongst young widows and their children. In 1969, the Society of Compassionate Friends began it's ministry amongst bereaved parents. Both organisations are seeking to mobilise the community in it's care of the bereaved. This is a corporate responsibility to be shared equally between the specialist team and the community. Such organisations as these are pioneering a completely new approach to the whole subject of bereavement.

The aura of obscenity which contemporary society had built around Death and Bereavement is being broken down—even though rather slowly—and traditional taboos are being swept aside. At long last this crisis of mortality is being accepted and acknowledged, not as a problem for which the individual must find a solution, but as an exercise in community therapy.

Death is inevitable, but not it's consequences. In the words of Lord Milner: 'We owe it to the dead not to let ourselves be crushed, saddened we must be, but not broken. Not weaker or less resolute to fight out to the end what is truly the Battle of Life.'

7

IN SEARCH OF A SOLUTION

It is with a sense of sincere happiness, I would say,
that your Society (of Compassionate Friends), is not
only a timely, but a necessary 'key' to unlock the
closed and barred minds, entrapped in the eternal
marshes of grief. Although the eventual goal appears
far off, the Ark to cross the void has been launched!
                              M. J. Narasimhan Jr.

WE have followed the story of Margaret and Peter Robinson
from beginning to end. From the moment Joe ran downstairs in his new school uniform we were able to share his
parents pride and self-satisfaction. And when he was
admitted to Greenhill District Hospital we were able to
share the anxiety of his mother and the medical staff.
Then the unexpected and the terrible happened. Joe
died. What could we do? Helplessly, we watched the
Robinsons plunge into the depths of grief and observed
their inability to share their sorrow even with their closest
relatives and friends. Step by step we have followed
Margaret through her bereavement experience, and we
have seen something of her feelings and reactions.

We have watched the caring team or the 'professionals'
as they were called, attempting to help the couple despite
their own limitations. We have examined some of the
reasons behind contemporary society's taboo on death.
There can be few of us who, having read of the Robinsons'
plight, would find it difficult to recall similar incidents in
our own lives, times when we have failed others when they
most needed our help.

Despite all the hinderances in their path, Margaret and Peter Robinson survived the loss of Joe . . . but only just! And their matrimonial and mental survival can only be attributed to the care which they rather belatedly received.

It would be quite wrong to bring this book to a conclusion on an optimistic note. The fact that the residents of No 22 Mickleforth Terrace did survive their ordeal was luck rather than good management. I hope that, in some small way the needs of the bereaved have been highlighted. The need for further action is obvious. But what action, and when. The letters pour into the few organisations attempting to cope with the probelm of bereavement. A glance at some of the letters might help to indicate some of the areas of concern. A letter from New Zealand told a sad tale. The previous Autumn, the writer told us, he had lost not only his wife, but his children and mother as well, in an airline disaster at Toronto, Canada. He had lost, as if in the twinkling of an eye, all that he ever really loved. Overnight his home ceased to have any meaning. He was completely along and broken.

His need was a special one. He wished to share his grief, not just by writing a lengthy letter, but by contacting somebody else who had been bereaved as a result of the same crash. Friends back home just could not understand him—nor he them. They could not share his grief because it was too overwhelming. They were appalled by the tragedy. It left them speechless. Silent! After some research, and with the help of national newspapers, an American family bereaved in the same airline disaster was located and introductions made. The New Zealander and the Americans shared their mutual grief and in it's sharing they found—at long last—peace of mind.

Not all stories are quite so dramatic, although they are all extremely sad. There was the couple from Texas whose only child had died as the result of an 'automobile' accident.

Like Joe, he was the 'apple of their eye' and when he died they ceased to live. Life was now a burden and somehow 'the folks back home just didn't understand'. There were flowers by the dozen at his graveside and letters of sympathy crowded the back room, but nobody had time to listen! It was all go! One day, whilst Mrs Z was under a hair-dryer in a neighbour's home, she saw an article about the Society of the Compassionate Friends in a magazine she was reading.

The following week she wrote a sixteen page letter to the Society. She was unable to share her grief with her husband for fear of hurting him any further. 'You can see the pain written in his eyes', she wrote, 'but we can't seem to help one another!' She blamed the lad who had loaned the car to her son. She blamed the emergency services for not reaching the scene of the accident quickly enough and she blamed herself for her impatience and intolerance towards her teenage son when he was alive! As the weeks passed her letters lost some of their bitterness. They were not quite so long either. Instead of dwelling solely on her own guilt and remorse she began to introduce other topics into her letters. Was Nixon right with his Vietnam policy and did the Apollo launch pad in Florida really merit quite so many dollars being spent on it? Letters bounced back and forth across the Atlantic. Somehow, she found it helped to be able to write to somebody who didn't really know her. Somebody who wasn't living in her immediate vicinity . . . yet somebody she could rely on to understand how she felt. A year later, fifty-four letters later, Mrs Z found herself writing short witty letters scarcely a page long. Her son was seldom mentioned now. She hadn't forgotten him. How could she? And she knew that her correspondent in England had not forgotten either. But a depth of understanding had at last been reached which had no need for words.

She seldom writes to England now. She has no need to!

Those letters have purged her of most of her bitterness and she now feels able to lead a normal life. Her husband, after a nervous breakdown, is returning to work, and they have been able to laugh together as they used to do. She doesn't feel deserted by her friend on the other side of the Atlantic and she knows that when painful anniversaries arrive or things go wrong . . . all she has to do is to take out a pen and some paper.

Sometimes the pain of grief is almost overwhelming and tempts even the strongest to think of suicide. Not so very long ago a young man of twenty-three was swept to his death whilst fishing on the East coast of England. This was a bitter blow to his widowed mother. She loved him dearly, but her grief was shared with her married daughter who lived some thirty miles down the coast. Robert had always been a popular lad both at school and at university, from which he had graduated with an 'upper second' in Modern Languages. How proud his father would have been of him. His death aged his mother overnight. The neighbours were full of pity for her—but that was all.

As the months passed Mrs R resigned herself to her loss and turned her attention and love to her daughter, who was now expecting her first child. This was to be her first grandchild. She was to become a Grandmother! She never tired of telling her neighbours at the launderette. Yes, they knew all about it! And they were saving her their spare Green Shield stamps to enable her to buy the young couple a carry-cot!

Then the unexpected happened. Suddenly, out of the blue, disaster struck again. She found her daughter standing on the doorstep—case in hand. Her son-in-law had walked out on her. 'He's with another woman, mum.' Tears drowned the rest of her explanation as her ageing mother put an arm round her and took her inside. 'Come on lass, it's not the end of the world', she remarked. But it was for her daughter! She just couldn't cope. She travelled miles in search of her husband. She just had to get him back. Wasn't his baby due within six weeks? But she didn't find him, and even her appeals to him in the personal column of the local newspaper were a failure. The girl was heart broken. Her mother struggled on, despite everything, and tried to keep a smile on her face. And then tragedy struck for a third time. Returning with aching arms from a weekly shopping expedition Mrs R opened the front door to find her daughter in a collapsed state lying on the hall floor. In her hand was an empty tablet bottle . . . on the mantel piece was a letter explaining everything. The emergency services did everything possible to save the young girl's life, but she died and her baby with her.

Words cannot adequately describe the hell which Mrs R went through. Within a very short time she had made an attempt on her own life but only after a cry for help had been sent to the Society—which she had read about in a woman's magazine. Within a very short time of the receipt of her letter, all the voluntary and statutory services in her area had been told of her plight. Today, she is receiving every possible care and she is still alive, and once again has learnt to smile. Her courage is enormous, but it needed a little help.

Not all the people who benefit from expressing their grief in the written word are women. Letters are frequently sent in by men who find the loss of their wives almost unbearable. One such letter was received several days after a BBC/TV programme, 'Viewpoint', when reactions to death were openly discussed. Written by a man aged seventy, the letter described the relief which he had experienced when he had learnt from the programme that it was not a shameful thing to talk about the person whom one had lost in death.

It appeared that he was almost blackmailed into keeping

silent about his wife. He was made to feel ashamed whenever he mentioned his deceased wife in company. He writes, 'Certain people hand out that "click" about time heals and its best never to talk of the departed. Well, I don't want to forget and I am truly grateful for the remarks on the programme. I was made to feel that I was imposing on my friends if I ever talked about my late wife . . . and now you have given me the classic consolation plus the realisation that as she was lovely I am entitled to talk about her loveliness. Because of what you say I no longer feel it wrong to look at our "snaps" and think of when they were taken and all our personal happiness.' Ten pages in length, this letter voiced all the grief and sorrow of the contemporary widower, but through the sharing of his grief with somebody who would understand he discovered a new purpose in life.

Irrespective of whether the plea for help comes from New Zealand or Nottingham, it's content is the same. 'Please let me share this experience with you. My mind is so confused that I desperately need somebody who is prepared to sit and listen to me as I unravel my bruised memories yard by yard. It is going to be a painful experience for both of us, but unless you give me an opportunity to unravel the past and put it in perspective how can I face the future? People keep telling me to pull myself together. To snap out of it and forget the past. They say that time heals. But surely no wound will heal unless it has been purged of it's bitterness. I know that you will be embarrassed by my tears. I know that you will be bored, but please listen to me. Bitterness, you ask? Perhaps I mean self-reproach or shame. Whatever it is, I cannot carry this burden alone. The road is too steep and the pain too great. I shall only get to the top of the hill if I am able to lean on a firm shoulder whose strength lies in the reality of the feet which bear it's weight.'

The sharing of grief is the only solution to the crisis which surrounds bereavement in our age. To share a person's deepest sorrows is to accept their reality and to acknowledge the fact that none of us is immune from death. So long as we deny the reality and the inevitability of death in our own lives, we shall always hold ourselves back from that depth of involvement which involves or places us at risk.

The New Zealander, the Texan mother, the Lincolnshire widow who attempted suicide and the seventy year old widower were only helped because somebody heard their cry and was able to share their grief.

We all need to look closely at our own sometimes very secret reaction to the deaths in our midst. The story of Margaret and Peter Robinson is not unique. Somewhere in every town and village, in the office or on the factory floor you will find another Peter Robinson. You will find Margaret in the launderette, the supermarket and the bingo hall. Help them today. They need you.

THE CHRISTIAN HOPE

You should not grieve like the rest of men, who
have no hope.   1 Thess. 4, 13

THE gang still played football down Mickleforth Terrace.
Some voices were beginning to break. Other lads were
unmistakably longer in the leg and John Robinson had
taken his elder brother's place as hero of the street team.
He didn't play as well as Joe had done, but then he was his
brother's brother and this still meant a lot to the lads—
although they never mentioned it. Somehow when John
was keeping goal, they knew that they hadn't lost Joe after
all. He was still with them and in some indefinable way he
was urging them on to greater achievements . . who knows
they might win the League Cup yet!

A year had gone by, but very little seemed to have
changed along the Terrace. Even the roundsman's float
and the factory bus kept to their strict timetables. Since
Joe died another winter, spring and summer had come and
gone. The trees at the end of the street continued to carpet
the pavements with gold, as they had done for the last
fifty years, and as they would no doubt continue to do for
another hundred autumns. There would be changes, of
course. One day the gang would have to grow up, and the
factory bus would come to collect them. But they would
make quite sure that their own children, especially the
boys, would follow in their footsteps. The football would
always bounce at the end of the street.

In time, the little houses might be pulled down, but,
nothing could ever destroy what had become so precious to

the people who lived and worked in that tiny corner of the North of England. The spirit of Joe would live on in their lives and in the lives of their children after them. For with his death, Joe found freedom and fulfilment in the eternal pattern of his God.

The parish priest knew this, he longed to share this truth with Margaret and Peter, but somehow he felt he might hurt them! He had seen death many times before and active service in the Second World War had provided him with an opportunity to reflect upon the eternity of the Almighty. He remembered how, as a junior forces padre, he had spent one day ministering to the dying and the wounded on a battlefield in France. The day was hot. The sky blue. In his nostrils was the stench of death, and yet the vast expanse of sky reminded him of God's overall authority. God was in control. God did care, and there was a meaning to that battlefield and the young lives which had been given. They were important to God because they were his own!

Taking Margaret and Peter gently aside, the parish priest would point out to them the beauty of the universe, with it's infinite variety of colours shapes and smells. He would draw their attention to the glory of a winter sunset which bathed the Terrace in red light, and would show them the star filled sky. He would point to the great power stations—full of energy, full of strength, pouring light and life into the homes of our land. He would show them the splendour of Durham Cathedral where man's faith in God has produced a miracle in stone and glass, and he would show them the beaches of Northumberland whipped by a wild North Sea on an April evening—full of God's majesty and might. God was in all of these revealing himself to his children. Creation is not the work of a demented spirit, it is the masterpiece of a Creator who is concerned about everything and everyone!

It is in this context of the universality of God, that he would point to Margaret and Peter that life is God's greatest gift to us, and through our lives as lived on this earth each one of us is called to glorify God. We are called, irrespective of colour and creed by God to reflect his glory in the world—whether we live at No 22 Mickleforth Terrace or at Lambeth Palace. This is the greatest privilege that God can bestow upon any of his creatures.

It is true, he would say to Margaret, that Joe's life was short. Nobody could deny that—but these standards are Man's standards only—not God's. For whether one lives five years or one hundred years, in the eyes of God the 'days of man are but as grass'. Life is short, he would tell them, but each life, irrespective of it's length has an integral part to play in God's plan for the universe. Joe's life was not wasted. He had fulfilled his mission and he had now returned to his Creator. Only God can assess the contribution which any one life has made to his eternal purpose for the salvation of Mankind.

But it must not be thought that God is an impersonal force. That he has no feeling. Why else did God become incarnate in Jesus Christ? 'And the Word was made flesh, and dwelt among us, and we beheld his glory, the glory as of the only begotten of the Father, full of grace and truth.' He would tell the Robinsons that because God was the author of all life, he was concerned in the quality of the lives we lead. And to save man from his evil ways—for Man is a free creature and not a slave to an impersonal deity—he gave us his Son. There can be little doubt that, as a child, Jesus was not unlike the boys in the Mickleforth gang. He had his playmates and, in his formative years, he was moulded by the people around him. The carpenter's shop was a busy place. There were always lots of visitors. And as with Joe, Jesus made many friends! Just how many friends they would never know!

The parish priest realised that Margaret and Peter might neither agree nor understand what he was trying to say to them. The consolation and hope which the Christian Church can bring to those who mourn might be turned aside. But, he thought to himself, he would tell them that Jesus Christ came from a simple home and shared all those human emotions which can cause us so much pain. He too knew the agony of grief when a dearly loved person died. No one but Jesus could understand fully the depth of sorrow through which Mary Magdalene and Martha passed when their brother Lazarus died. We are told that when he saw Mary weeping, he was moved at the sight of her tears and he said in great distress, with a sigh from the heart, 'Where have you put him?' And we are told in verse 35, quite simply that 'Jesus wept'. Jesus knew no shame in weeping quite openly. He loved Lazarus. And if you lose somebody whom you love very much, you do weep. The priest only wished that he and a few more of his parishioners could weep openly with Margaret and so encourage and enable her to let her tears flow freely. He was glad that he had remembered the story about Lazarus, it was an important one!

Jesus Christ had known all the agonies of the heart through which the average man passes. Like Margaret and Peter when they found themselves alienated from society through Joe's death, Jesus too had experienced terrible moments of desolation and loneliness. Moments of great fear. In the Garden of Gethsemane, had he not prayed, 'O my Father, if it be possible, let his cup pass from me: nevertheless not as I will, but as thou wilt.' And on the Cross, hands and feet pinned with nails, a crude wreath of thorns thrust upon his forehead, had he not cried out, 'My God, my God, why hast thou forsaken me?' Yes, Jesus knew all about suffering and sorrow and by his short life gave meaning to it. Jesus was the sort of man a person like Peter Robinson could perhaps understand. But Margaret would ask, 'Why my Joe? Was it really so necessary for Joe to have to die so young.'

But death is not the end. It is merely a door through which every person must pass on their journey towards completion and fulfilment in Christ. And standing by that doorway is Jesus Christ who said, 'I am the Way, the Truth and the Life. I am the resurrection and the life; he that believeth in me, though he were dead, yet shall he live; And whosoever liveth and believeth in me shall never die.' The parish priest knew that if he could share this truth with the Robinsons, then they might discover that peace of mind which only God can give.

And that is just what he did!

On the first anniversary of Joe's death, the parish priest made a point of visiting Margaret and Peter late in the evening when all the family had gone to bed. It had been a difficult day for them. First anniversaries always are! The day had begun badly with Peter missing the shift bus and had seemingly ended disastrously when Clare, who was now almost three, had fallen downstairs, badly cutting her top lip.

Margaret had spent the day quietly at home re-living every minute of that sad day a year ago which so changed their lives. In her mind's eye, she saw Peter standing at the door with the young policeman at his side, she saw Joe's pale but composed face on the hospital pillow she saw the funeral and all those flowers. God, it had been a terrible day! And not even a neighbour had found the time or courage to interrupt her thoughts and share a cup of tea with her. Then the vicar arrived. Margaret had almost had enough! It had been a bad day and she wanted to forget it and go to bed.

Surprised at the arrival of her unexpected visitor, Margaret nevertheless made a pot of tea. And then, quite suddenly and rather to their astonishment, the Robinsons found themselves listening to all that the vicar had to say. For the very first time, he encouraged them to look at the world about them. He spoke of God's creative skill and of the role of Jesus Christ within the universe. He spoke of Joe and of the freedom of the spirit which death had brought him. Indeed, that night he spoke of a great many things to the Robinsons. For the very first time Margaret and Peter shared their grief *together*.

It was 2 a.m. A chill early morning wind whistled through the Terrace. A dustbin lid rolled. A child coughed in a nearby house. Grey streaks began to climb across the night sky as if to meet the dawn. The Robinsons went to bed. The bedroom lights at No 22 flickered, and finally went out. The street was asleep.

ANTHOLOGY

WORDS OF COMFORT AND COMPASSION

An anthology of prose and poems from every age for those who mourn and for those who care for them—selected by the bereaved.

Well, everyone can master grief but he that has it.

Much Ado About Nothing (Act 2)

FROM THE BIBLE

You are dust, and to dust you shall return. Gen. 3.19

The eternal God is your dwelling place, And underneath are the everlasting arms.   Deut. 33.27

The Lord is my shepherd, I shall not want; he makes me to lie down in green pastures.   Ps. 23.1

I lift up my eyes to the hills. For whence does my help come?
My help comes from the Lord, who made heaven and earth.

Ps. 121.1

The Lord heals the brokenhearted, and binds up their wounds.   Ps. 147:3

For I know that my Redeemer lives, and at last he will stand upon the earth; and after my skin has been thus destroyed, then from my flesh I shall see God.

Job 19.25, 26.

He will feed his flock like a shepherd, and he will gather the lambs in his arms, he will crry them in his bosom, and gently lead those that are with young.   Isa. 40.11.

For you shall go out in joy, and be led forth in peace; the mountains and hills before you shall break forth into singing, and all the trees of the field shall clap their hands.
Isa. 55.12.

Blessed be the God and Father of our Lord Jesus Christ! By his great mercy we have been born anew to a living hope through the resurrection of Jesus Christ from the dead.   1 Pet 1.3

Peace I leave with you; my peace I give to you; not as the world gives do I give to you. Let not your hearts be troubled, neither let them be afraid.   John 14.27

Watch therefore, for you do not know on what day your Lord is coming.   Matt. 24.42

Lo! I tell you a mystery. We shall not all sleep, but we shall all be changed, in the twinkling of any eye, at the last trumpet.   1 Cor. 15.51

For I am sure that neither death, nor life, nor angels nor principalities . . . will be able to separate us from the love of God in Christ Jesus our Lord.   Rom. 8.38

The Lord is at hand. Have no anxiety about anything, but in everything by prayer and supplication with thanksgiving let your requests be made known to God.   Phil. 4.6

So we do not lose heart. Though our outer nature is wasting away, our inner nature is being renewed every day. For this slight momentary affliction is preparing us for an eternal weight of glory beyond all comparison.
2 Cor. 4.16

But we would not have you ignorant, brethren, concerning those who are asleep, that you may not grieve as others do who have no hope.   1 Thess. 4.13

They shall hunger no more, neither thirst any more; the sun shall not strike them nor any heat. For the Lamb in the midst of the throne shall be their shepherd, and he will guide them to springs of living waters; and God will wipe away every tear from their eyes.   Rev. 7.16, 17

After this I looked, and behold, a great multitude which no man could number, from every nation, from all tribes and peoples and tongues, standing before the throne and before the Lamb clothed in white robes.   Rev. 7.10

For the love of Christ controls us, because we are convinced that one has died for all; therefore all have died. And he died for all, that those who live might live no longer for themselves but for him who for their sake died and was raised.   2 Cor. 5.14

And all the angels stood round the throne and round the elders and they worshipped God saying 'Amen! Blessing and glory and wisdom and thanksgiving be to our God for ever and ever.'   Rev. 7.11, 12

(quotations are taken from the R S V)

POEMS AND PROSE

Think of me as withdrawn to dimness,
Your's still—You mine.
Remember all the best of our past moments,
And forget the rest. And so where I gently wait,
Come gently on.   William Allingham

They shall not grow old, as we that are left grow old: Age shall not weary them, nor the years condemn. At the going

down of the sun and in the morning. We will remember
them.   Laurence Binyon 1869–1943
(from *Poems for the Fallen*)

The door of death is made of gold,
That mortal eyes cannot behold;
But when the mortal eyes are closed,
And cold and pale the limbs reposed.
The soul awakes, and, wondering sees
In her mild hand the Golden Keys;
The Grave is Heaven's Golden Gate,
And rich and poor around it wait;
O Shepherdess of England's fold,
Behold this Gate of Pearl and Gold.
                              William Blake 1757–1827

What I find so often is that people should have been taught
about death when they were full of sap and life, and when
they could still face death not as a terror but as a challenge.
                              Archbishop Bloom

What is dying? I am standing on the sea shore. A ship sails
to the morning breeze and starts for the ocean. She is an
object of beauty and I stand watching her till at last she
fades on the horizon, and someone at my side says, 'She is
gone.' Gone where? Gone from my sight, that is all; she is
just as large in the masts, hull and spars as she was when
I saw her, and just as able to bear her load of living freight
to it's destination.

The diminished size and total loss of sight is in me, not
in her; and just at the moment when someone at my side
says, 'She is gone.' there are others who are watching her
coming, and other voices take up a glad shout, 'There she
comes' and that is dying.   Bishop C. H. Brent 1862–1929

After this it was noised abroad that Mr Valiant-for-Truth
was taken with a summons by the same post as the other,
and had this for a token that the summons was true, that

his pitcher was broken at the fountain. When he understood it, he called for his friends and told them of it. Then said he, 'I am going to my fathers, and tho' with great difficulty I am got hither, yet now I do not repent me of all the trouble I have been at to arrive where I am. My sword I give to him that shall succeed me in my pilgrimage, and my courage and skill to him that can get it. My marks and my scars I carry with me, to be a witness for me, that I have fought his battles who now will be my rewarder.

When the day that he must go hence was come, many accompanied him to the riverside, into which as he went he said, 'Death, where is thy sting?' And as he went down deeper he said, 'Grave, where is thy victory?' So he passed over, and all the trumpets sounded for him on the other side.   John Bunyan 1628–1688
(from *Pilgrim's Progress*)

So just as a good mariner when he draws near to the harbour lets down his sails, and enters it gently with slight headway on; so we ought to let down the sails of our worldly pursuits, and turn to God with all our understanding and heart, so that we may come to that haven with all composure and all peace. And our own nature gives us a good lesson in gentleness, in so far as there is in such a death no pain, nor any bitterness; but as a ripe apple lightly and without violence detaches itself from it's bough, so our soul severs itself without suffering from the body where it has dwelt.   Dante
(from *A Book of Peace*, Elizabeth Goudge)

Death be not proud, though some have called thee Mighty and dreadful, for, thou art not so, For those, whom thou think'st thou dost overthrow, Die not, poor death.
                                    John Donne 1571–1631
(from *Holy Sonnets*)

Then Almitra spoke, saying, We would ask now of death.
And he said:
If you would indeed behold the spirit of death, open your
heart wide unto the body of life.
For life and death are one, even as the river and sea are one.
In the depths of your hopes and desires lies your silent
knowledge of the beyond. And like seeds dreaming beneath
the snow, your heart dreams of spring. Trust the dreams,
for in them is hidden the gate to eternity. Your fear of death
is but the trembling of the shepherd when he stands before
the King whose hand is to be laid upon him in honour.
Is not the shepherd not joyful beneath his trembling, that
he shall wear the mark of the king?
Yet is he not more mindful of his trembling? For what is it
to die but to stand naked in the wind and to melt into the
sun. And what is it to cease breathing but to free the
breath from it's breathless tides, that it may rise and
expand and seek God unencumbered?
Only when you drink from the river of silence shall you
indeed sing. And when you have reached the mountain top,
then you shall begin to climb.
And when the earth shall claim your limbs, then you shall
truly dance.   Kahlil Gilran
                                              (from *The Prophet*)

So be my passing!
My task accomplished and the long day done,
My wages taken, and in my heart
Some late lark singing,
Let me be gathered to the quiet west,
The sundown splendid and serene,
Death.   William Henley 1849–1903
                                        (from *Margaritae Sorori*)

Death is nothing at all—I have only slipped away into the

next room. I am I and you are you. Whatever we were to each other, that we are still. Call me by my old familiar name, speak to me in the easy way which you always used. Put no difference into your tone; wear no forced air of solemnity or sorrow. Laugh as we always laughed at the little jokes we enjoyed together. Play, smile, think of me, pray for me. Let my name be the household word that it always was. Let it be spoken without effort, without the ghost of a shadow in it. Life means all that it ever meant. It is the same as it ever was; there is absolutely unbroken continuity. What is this death but a negligible accident. Why should I be out of your mind because I am out of your sight?

I am but waiting for you, for an interval, some where very near just around the corner. All is well. Nothing is past; nothing is lost. One brief moment and all will be as it was before.   Henry Scott Holland 1847–1918

I am ready to make the great journey. My trunks are packed. I can go at any time.   Pope John XXIII

God created me to do Him some definite service; He has committed some work to me which He has not committed to another. I have my mission. I may never know it in this life but I shall be told it in the next.

I am a link in a chain, a bond of connection between persons. He has not created me for naught. I shall do good, I shall do his work. I shall be an angel of peace, a preacher of truth in my own place while not intending it—if I do but keep his commandments. Therefore I will trust him. Whatever, wherever I am, I can never be thrown away. If I am in sickness, my sickness may serve him; in perplexity, my perplexity may serve him; if in sorrow, my sorrow may serve him. He does nothing in vain. He knows what he is about. He may take away my friends. He may throw me among strangers. He may make me feel desolate, make my spirits sink, hide my future from me—still He knows what he is about.   Cardinal Newman 1801–1890

Man is a sacred city, built of marvellous earth,
Life was lived nobly here to give this body birth,
Something was in this brain and in this eager hand.
Death is so dumb and blind, death cannot understand.
Death drifts the brain with dust and soils the young limbs' glory.
Death makes woman a dream, and men a traveller's story.
Death drives the lovely soul to wander under the sky,
Death opens unknown doors. It is most grand to die.

John Masefield 1878–1967
(from *The Centurions*)

For the Christian, then, death is not a calamity, a leap in the dark, or just the end of a happy life. It is the gateway into a fuller and more wonderful experience. We have seen how God has looked upon our sad estate, made it possible for us to enter into life, and given us the assurance of dwelling with him hereafter. But we have also seen that his happy outcome will not take place in the natural course of events; it depends upon our receiving by an act of decision what God offers to us. Let us beware of missing this gift through failure on our part to do what is necessary to secure so great a prize.   Talbot Mohan
(from *Your Bereavement*)

They that love beyond the world cannot be separated by it. Death cannot kill what never dies. Nor can spirits ever be divided, they love and live in the same divine principle; the root and record of their friendship.

William Penn 1644–1718
(from *Union of Friends*)

Swiftly, without warning, snatched away before our eyes!
When we witness sudden death we come to realise,
How near we are to the eternal—closer than we know,
Nearer than we dream each day as on our way we go.
Knowing not how often we approach the Borderline,
Stumbling in our blindness on the edge of things divine,
Transient is human life, and frail the mortal bond,
But God is love, and friends are waiting in the world beyond.

Patience Strong
(from *Sudden Death*)

Speak to him, thou, for he hears and spirit with spirit can meet.
Closer is he than breathing, and nearer than hands and feet.   Alfred Lord Tennyson 1809–1892

So death will come to fetch you?
No, not death, but God himself.
Death is not the horrible spectre we see represented in pictures.
The catechism teaches that death is the separation of the soul from the body; that is all.
I am not afraid of a separation which will unite me for ever with God.   St Theresa

Bereavement does not separate us from the love of God—only sin separates us from God. Christ who underwent every loss and grief ever experienced by mankind, is near to us and understands our sorrow.
I am convinced that the Holy Spirit enlightens the bereaved soul and gradually shows it how to re-arrange life. We are never forsaken by the Father who created us, by God the Son who bought us at such great cost to Himself and by God the Holy Spirit who sanctifies us.   K. Wootton

Love is not changed by death and nothing is lost and all in the end is harvest.   Edith Sitwell

If I should die and leave you here awhile,
Be not like others, sore undone, who keep
Long vigils by the silent dust, and weep.
For my sake, turn again to life and smile,
Nerving thy heart and trembling hand to do
Something to comfort weaker hearts than thine.
Complete those dear unfinished tasks of mine,
And I perchance may therein comfort you.

A. Price Hughes
(from *A Warrior on Wings*)

Though I am dead, grieve not for me with tears,
Think not of death with sorrowing and tears,
I am so near that every tear you shed touches and tortures
me, though you think me dead.
But when you laugh and sing in glad delight, my soul is
lifted upward to the light.
Laugh and be glad for all that life is giving and I,
though dead will share your joy in living.   Anon.

ACKNOWLEDGEMENTS

The author and publishers are grateful to the following for permission to quote extracts from:

Your Bereavement by Talbot Mohan (Hodder & Stoughton); *Man's Concern with Death* edited by Arnold Toynbee (Hodder & Stoughton); *The Prophet* by Kahlil Gilran (Knopf); 'The Seekers', The Society of Authors as the literary representative of the Estate of John Masefield; *Sudden Death* by Patience Strong; 'A Warrior on Wings' by A. Price-Hughes; *A Book of Peace* by Elizabeth Goudge (Michael Joseph).

Permission to quote from the *Jerusalem Bible* has been granted by Darton, Longman and Todd Ltd; extracts from the Revised Standard Version Bible are copyright and reproduced by permission.

ACKNOWLEDGMENTS

BIBLIOGRAPHY

Life begins at Death Leslie D. Weatherhead (Denholm House Press).
Your Bereavement Talbot Mohan (Hodder and Stoughton).
Yonder: A Little Book for the Bereaved Leslie Church (Epworth Press 1962).
One, of Great Price Sergei Hackel (Darton, Longman and Todd 1965).
A Grief Observed C. S. Lewis (Faber 1961).
The Valley of the Shadows H. Lilje (SCM 1950).
Christus Consolatur H. C. G. Moule (SPCK 1915).
In My Father's House Richard Tatlock (Mowbray 1956).
The Loved One E. Waugh (Penguin Books 1952)
On the Death of A Child John G. Williams (SPCK 1965).
We Die unto the Lord Pierre Herbin (Challoner 1960).
Dying we Live Edited by T. Huddleston (Fontana 3rd imp. 1962).
Holy Living: Holy Dying Jeremy Taylor (Longmans Green 1941).
Interpreting the Cross Max Warren (SCM 1966).
Death and Those We Love Alix and George Reindorp (Mothers Union 1963).
The Resurrection of Christ A. M. Ramsey (Fontana 1961).
Death and After W. K. Lowther Clarke (SPCK Chichester Pamphlets).
Margaret J. D. Ross (Hodder and Stoughton 1963).
The Four Last Things H. Williams (Mowbray 1960).
A Very Easy Death Simone de Beauvoir (Deutch, Weidenfeld and Nicholson 1966).
Grief and How to Overcome It Sarah Morris (Allen and Unwin 1971).
You and Your Grief E. Jackson (Channel Press 1961).
Letters of Spiritual Counsel and Guidance John Keble (Mowbrays 1920).
The Spiritual Letters of Archbishop Fenelon H. S. Lear (Longmans 1894).
Select Letters St Jerome (Heinemann 1954).
Spiritual Letters of Father Congreve (Mowbrays 1928).
The Pastoral Care of the Dying Norman Autton (SPCK)
The Pastoral Care of the Bereaved Norman Autton (SPCK).
Le Chretien et La Mort Karl Rahner (Desclee de Brouwer 1966).
Tout le Reste est Silence Jean Montaurier (Librairie Plon 1969).
La Souffrance pourquoi? Louis Retif (Editions du Centurion 1966).
La Mort . . . et puis apres? Marc Oraison (Le Signe/Fayard 1967).
L'Imitation de N.S. Jesus Christ (Editions Arts et Metiers Graphiques).
Der Kreuzweg unseres Herrn Romano Guardini (Matthias–Grunewald–Mainz).

Parish Prayers Edited Frank Colquhoun (Hodder and Stoughton 1967).
A Chain of Prayer Across the Ages Selina Fitzherbert Fox (Murray 1963).

Death, Grief and Mouring G. Gorer (Cresset 1965).
Man's Concern with Death A. Toynbee & Others (Hodder and Stoughton 1968).
Dying, Death and Disposal Edited by Gilbert Cope (SPCK 1970).
Bereavement—Death—The Funeral Edited by Simon Doniger (Pastoral Psychology Press, New York 1955).
An Approach to Community Mental Health Gerald Caplan (Tavistock Publications).
Dying John Hinton (Penguin Books 1967).
Ministering to the Grief Sufferer C. C. Bacbmann (Prentice-Hall 1964).
Awareness of Dying Glaser and Strauss (Weidenfeld & Nicholson 1965).
The Role of the Clergyman in Time of Crisis R. H. Felix (University of Florida 1963).

ARTICLES

The Sorrows of Bereavement, B. H. Becker *Journal of Abnormal and Social Psychology* (27 1933, pp. 391–410).
Bereavement and Grief Work, C. Benda *Journal of Pastoral Care* XVI (Spring 1962 No 1, pp. 1–13).
Childhood Mourning and Its Implications for Psychiatry, J. Bowlby *American Journal of Psychiatry* (118 1961, pp. 481–98).
Depression and Childhood Bereavement, F. Brown *Journal of Mental Science* (107 1961, pp. 754–777).
When They Miss a Father Most, Kate Wharton *Daily Telegraph* (21st May 1965).
Loneliness, J. Cohen *Family Doctor* (December 1964).
The British Way of Death, G. Gorer *Sunday Times* (15th November 1964).
Effects of Bereavement on Physical and Mental Health, C. M. Parkes *British Medical Journal* (1st August 1964, pp. 274f).
Grief as Illness, C. M. Parkes *New Society*, 80, (9th April 1964).
Recent Bereavement as a Cause of Mental Illness, C. M. Parkes *British Journal of Psychiatry* Vol. 110, 465, (March 1965).
Bereavement and Mental Illness, C. M. Parkes *British Journal of Medical Psychology* (1965) 39, I.
'Seeking' and 'Finding' a Lost Object, C. M. Parkes *Soc. Sci. & Med.* (1970) Vol. 4, pp. 187–201.
Broken Heart: A Statistical Study of Increased Mortality among Widowers, C. M. Parkes *et al. Brit. Med. Journal* (22nd March 1969, I, pp. 740–643).

The First Year of Bereavement, C. M. Parkes *Journal for the Study of Interpersonal Processes* 33, (4th November 1970).

Psycho-Social Transitions, C. M. Parkes *Soc. Sci. & Med.* (5, 1971, pp. 101–115).

Grief, B. H. Pentney *Nursing Times* (12th November 1964, pp. 1946–8).

Grief and Mourning, Symposium *Contact* (12th October 1964).

Community Care of the Widow, A. Torrie *British Medical Journal* (23rd April 1960).

Death of a Child, Moira Keenan *The Times* (16th November 1970.)

When Times Alone Cannot Heal, William Purcell *Good Housekeeping* (December 1971).

Bereavement and Care of the Bereaved, Simon Stephens *Midwife and Health Visitor* (Vol. 8, No. 3, March 1972).